Help!
I'm in Love with
a *Narcissist*

Help!
I'm in Love with
a *Narcissist*

STEVEN CARTER AND JULIA SOKOL

M. Evans and Company, Inc.
New York

M. Evans and Company, Inc.
216 East 49th Street
New York, NY 10017

Library of Congress Cataloging-in Publication Data

Carter, Steven
  Help! I'm in love with a narcissist / Steven Carter and Julia Sokol.
    p. cm.
  ISBN 1-59077-077-3 (hardcover)
  1. Narcissism. 2. Man-woman relationships. I. Sokol, Julia. II. Title.
  BF575.N35C365 2005   158.2—dc22   2004019359

Book design and typeformatting by Bernard Schleifer

Printed in the United States of America

9 8 7 6 5 4 3 2 1

To Carla, who always makes us laugh.

In memory of Gus, whose devotion and bravery we will never forget.

CONTENTS

TO OUR READERS

We are writers, not therapists. Our insights come primarily from our own experiences and from the experiences of countless men and women who struggle with many variations of the conflicts described in this book.

Therefore, we want to make it clear that this book is not meant to be a substitute for professional psychological help. It is not our intention to diminish our information and experience, or to diminish the information shared by those we have interviewed. But we do need to emphasize its limitations. Every person's struggle is unique and deserving of individual attention and examination. This book is intended to provide a starting point in that process.

ACKNOWLEDGMENTS

A book like this is never possible without help and support. We'd like to thank first all the people who have shared their relationship stories with us over the years. They have been wonderfully helpful. We're especially grateful to the men and women who took the time to find our site on the Internet and respond to our requests.

We want to thank our editor, PJ Dempsey, for her experience, expertise, and kindness. We'd also like to thank her for always being first with some of the dumbest and funniest jokes making the rounds via e-mail. We'd also like to thank Harry McCullough, for all his publishing know-how. And we want to thank all the other folks at M. Evans, including Dina Jordan, Evan Johnston, Mary Boughton, and Matt Harper.

We always need to thank our agent Barbara Lowenstein, who is a walking definition of what it means to be the consummate professional.

Friends are a great thing. We'd both especially like to thank Susan Hauptman and Leonard Post for all their encouragement, support, and advice. We don't want to forget Wendy Gladding, Jeff Gladding, and Keely Varada.

We also want to thank Don Schimelfenig and Jill Carter for all their understanding and support. And we can't do a book without including the creatures with whom we share and have shared our space—Huck, Harry, Holly, Maggie, Max the kitten, Max the black Persian, Carla the dog, Carla the cat, Gus, and Fuji.

Finally our saddest and most heartfelt thank you. For many years George DeKay, the publisher of M. Evans, was our editor. He died soon after we started working on this project. George was profoundly smart, sane, and funny. He gave us almost twenty years of unwavering support, guidance, and kindness. He was the best, and we wish we could tell him in person how much we miss him and all his bow ties.

Part 1

ARE YOU IN LOVE WITH A NARCISSIST?

One

NARCISSISM—THE RELATIONSHIP ISSUE OF OUR TIMES

HAVEN'T MOST OF US BEEN HURT, SOMETIMES BADLY, by a romantic partner's over-the-top level of self-involvement? Haven't we all wondered why and how a loved one could be so oblivious to our feelings? Self-absorption is so prevalent that many say that we live in a narcissistic culture and are part of a narcissistic age. It is probably true that we are all at least a little bit more self-absorbed than we should be and that our relationships suffer accordingly. But some romantic partners are so narcissistic that they appear unredeemably destructive.

It's easy to "fall" for a narcissist. They can be very charismatic and usually engender strong emotions. They like to think of themselves as special, and at the beginning of a relationship, they will frequently draw us into their world and make us feel as though we are equally unique. That's why getting involved with a narcissist can be such a heady, whirlwind experience. Falling in love with a narcissist is easy, but the problems of building a workable, long-term relationship with such a person can seem almost insurmountable.

Consider the following stories about two separate relationships. Outwardly they appear quite different, but when you reflect on the underlying dynamics, you will begin to see the similarities.

MAGGIE AND JERRY

Maggie met Jerry soon after she joined an Internet dating service. She was attracted to Jerry's profile because he described himself as a "nice guy" who was tired of the dating scene. His profile revealed that he worked in the food industry, liked poetry and music, and went to the gym several times a week. Maggie also liked the photographs posted with his profile. There was one of him in a baseball cap, another of him standing next to a bicycle, and third of him with a little girl (who turned out to be his daughter) on his lap.

Jerry's profile said that he was romantic and intense, and that at thirty-seven, he was ready for the "real thing." So Maggie e-mailed him. He responded, and after a week of super-cute exchanges and notes, they made a phone date. They hit it off immediately, talking for almost two hours, mostly about Jerry's dream of owning his own restaurant, his interest in politics, and how he planned to run for office some day. Maggie loved hearing about his passions and his dreams. He sounded very interesting and exciting.

One of the things Maggie liked best about Jerry was his ability to open up and talk personally about his life. He immediately told Maggie about his failed marriage and how much he loved and missed living with his daughter. He said that his ex-wife was vindictive and that he didn't feel that he got to spend as much time with his daughter as he wanted.

On their first date, Jerry told Maggie that he couldn't get over how pretty she was and how smart. He said he hadn't expected to meet anybody on the Internet that he liked as much as he liked her. He asked her briefly about her job as a nurse, saying that he was very impressed that she had a job that helped others. He looked into her eyes when he told her, "I could sure use somebody like you in my life." When they left the coffee shop and headed for the dark parking lot, Maggie expected Jerry to walk her to her car and was taken aback when he didn't offer to do so. Maggie wondered if maybe that meant that he didn't like her as much as he said he did. But when Maggie checked her e-mail before going to bed, she found a note from Jerry saying that he thought they had an amazing connection and she was an "extraordinary woman—really special." They made a date for the following weekend.

Within a very short time, Jerry told Maggie that he thought they could be together forever and he couldn't get over how kind and thoughtful she was. From Maggie's point of view, with the exception of a few bad moments, the beginning of the relationship was wonderful and like a dream come true. Sometimes Jerry seemed inconsiderate (as in the parking lot episode), but Maggie decided it wasn't worth making a fuss. They had such a strong sexual and emotional connection. *Soul mates*, Maggie thought. *We're soul mates.*

It took Jerry less than six weeks to say "I love you," and Maggie was happy to say it back. Right after that, Jerry told Maggie he thought they should exchange apartment keys. Maggie was thrilled and quickly had one made for him. However, when she handed it to him a few days later, he said he hadn't gotten around to making one for her.

They were dating only a couple of months when Jerry told Maggie that he wanted her to meet his daughter, Callie; they quickly made plans to pick up Callie on Saturday and take her to lunch and to the mall. At the last minute, Jerry said that he had to work, and while he could have lunch with them, he asked Maggie if she minded taking Callie to the mall alone. Maggie was surprised that Jerry didn't insist on rearranging his work schedule so he could be with his little girl. However, she was also to spend the time with the child and wanted to prove that she could have a good relationship with his daughter.

When it was time for Callie to go home, Jerry phoned Maggie on her cell phone and said he was still tied up; could she take his little girl home. Maggie couldn't believe that Jerry wanted her and his ex-wife to meet. "Are you sure it's okay?" she asked. "Sure," he said. "Let her see what a beautiful woman looks like." Maggie expected that Jerry's ex-wife would be hard-edged and unpleasant, but instead the woman appeared good-natured and friendly. At the door, Callie told her mother about the day at the mall and showed her the book Maggie had bought her. Jerry's ex-wife hesitated and then asked her daughter to wait for a minute because she wanted to talk to Maggie privately.

"You look like a nice person," she said to Maggie. "So I just want to tell you to watch out because the only person Jerry cares about is Jerry."

Maggie didn't tell Jerry about the encounter; she didn't want to upset him or create problems for his relationship with his daughter. But she wondered if there was any truth to his ex-wife's statement. She also couldn't help but wonder if Jerry was deriving some kind of pleasure from having the two women meet.

Soon thereafter, Jerry and Maggie were supposed to go to Maggie's cousin's wedding, but that day Jerry appeared to purposely do everything he could to make sure they were late. Then, when they got there, he drank too much and was barely civil to anyone. They returned to Maggie's apartment, where they had their first fight. Maggie told him that she was hurt by the way he embarrassed her in front of her family. She expected Jerry to apologize and make up. Instead he screamed at her, "Your cousin is a boring jerk, and who do you think you are, telling me what I should do?" He then stormed out the door.

Maggie, who had never seen Jerry get angry, was stunned. She cried herself to sleep. At six A.M., her doorbell rang. It was an almost remorseful Jerry. "I'm sorry," he said. "I shouldn't have raised my voice. But you shouldn't have made me go someplace I didn't want to go." Maggie wanted to make up, but she was still upset. What she had liked most about the relationship was the sense that Jerry wanted to please her. What she was seeing, however, was a whole other side of Jerry. She also couldn't help remembering that although Jerry treated her home and her belongings as though they were his, he had never gotten around to giving her the key to his apartment.

As the relationship progressed, Maggie noticed other things that disturbed her. Jerry began to complain about her job and started saying mean things like, "Are you sure you're not bringing diseases home?" And Maggie started to realize that she couldn't get Jerry to pay attention to anything that was important to her. He appeared totally disinterested, and there were times when he acted as though she didn't exist. If she tried to force him to pay attention, he got angry.

Because Maggie wanted to improve the relationship, she brought home some brochures on the Florida Keys. She was sure that a few relaxing days alone together would be good for them. Jerry seemed intrigued, and they made plans to go away for the long President's Day weekend. Maggie was looking forward to it. Then, one week before they were going to leave, Jerry said that he changed his mind and decided that he needed some time by himself. Maggie was so disappointed that she started to cry. Jerry yelled at her, "Do you mean that I can't be alone when I need to be alone? Are you telling me what I can and can't do?"

More Questions than Answers

Currently, Maggie is miserable. She doesn't understand what is going on. Is Jerry getting scared of making a commitment? Did she do something to turn him off? Why did everything change? Maggie can't stop thinking about the relationship and everything that has happened. Did she do something wrong? How could he be this mean? How could he hurt her like this? Doesn't he care about what she is feeling and what she must be going through? Is it possible that Jerry's ex-wife is right—that the only person Jerry cares about is Jerry? Is it possible that Jerry is a narcissist? And, if he is, what exactly does that mean for the future of their relationship? She cares about this man, but is she engaged in a struggle she can't win?

Over the years, ever since we began writing books about relationships and interviewing men and women for these projects, we've heard variations of all these questions. We've listened to hundreds and hundreds of men and women who have been confused by partners who acted selfishly and self-involved. When we first started hearing stories about narcissistic romantic partners, almost inevitably these partners would be male. In fact, at one time it was generally believed that an overwhelming percentage of narcissists were male. Because women were considered more nurturing and less selfish, it seemed difficult to believe that the women who stayed home and put more emphasis on the needs of the family than they did on their own could be identified as narcissistic. But times have changed; women are out of the narcissistic closet. Here's an example of a relationship in which the woman is undeniably more narcissistic than her partner.

JEFF AND SHANNON

When Jeff met Shannon, he was thirty-five, and his friends and family had all but given up on his ever getting married. Yes, he had fallen in love before, but never with this level of intensity. As they say, Shannon totally set his world upside down. The first thing Jeff noticed about Shannon was the way she turned her head and smiled. Shannon had a killer smile. It made him weak in the knees. They met on a golf course and started their flirtation over drinks at the bar. Jeff was an attractive, single real-estate developer and man about town; Shannon, who was twenty-nine, had two children from her first marriage and was still married to her second husband.

As they sipped their margaritas, Shannon leaned into Jeff, her body brushing against his arm as she told him that she was trying to find a part-time job because she needed the money. It took him approximately fifteen minutes to remember that he needed "part-time" help in his office, three mornings a week.

Shannon showed up for work the following Wednesday morning, and by lunch time, she and Jeff were groping each other in the supply closet. The first few months of their relationship were insane, filled with clandestine meetings throughout the neighboring towns. In those moments when they were actually speaking, as opposed to shedding garments, Shannon told Jeff that her husband was controlling and emotionally abusive and that she couldn't take any more of his tyrannical screaming sessions. What she neglected to tell Jeff was that her husband was screaming over Shannon's various extramarital romances and flirtations, as well as her excessive drinking and over-the-top spending.

Shannon also implied that her husband had a "sexual problem" and said that they hadn't made love in over a year. "He must be crazy," Jeff told her. "Why do you stay with him?" Shannon told Jeff that she wanted to leave, but was scared. She was afraid her husband would conceal his money, and she was worried about how she and her eight-year-old twin sons (who were not his children) would manage. Jeff told her not to worry; if she got a divorce, he would marry her—on the spot. After they had this conversation, Jeff confided in his brother about the relationship. Jeff's brother promptly called their father, mother, and sister; they all converged at Jeff's condo to tell Jeff that he had lost his mind and that what he was doing wasn't right.

Jeff's sister said that she had friends who knew Shannon, and that Shannon was a selfish, self-involved mother who had already pulled her kids through one divorce and was now planning to do it all over again. Jeff's brother said that he thought Jeff should wait six months or a year just to see if his ardor cooled down. Jeff's parents said that they were trying to understand, but that it was difficult.

After speaking to his family, Jeff was conflicted and genuinely considering whether he should end the affair. That's when Shannon called him on her cell phone. She was crying, and she was sitting in her car in Jeff's driveway. Her husband had discovered that she was "in love with someone else." Shannon was afraid he was going to become "violent," so she had run out of the house in her nightgown, leaving the children with him. "Are you sure the kids will be okay?" Jeff asked. "Oh, yes," she answered. "He would never do anything to the twins."

Shannon spent the night at Jeff's apartment; by morning, they had a plan. Shannon would temporarily move into her sister's house while she looked for a place of her own to rent (which Jeff would pay for). Shannon would file for divorce, and as soon as the divorce was final, they would marry. The next day Jeff drove Shannon and her sister to Shannon's house to pick up her clothes and her kids.

Exactly a year later, Jeff found himself standing with Shannon in front of a judge, surrounded by friends and family. He sighed as he said the words, "I do." They had just bought a new, 3,000-square-foot house with an inground swimming pool, and Jeff was beginning to get a taste of what had upset her ex-husband.

"She is so beautiful that when I look at her, I want to do whatever she wants and give her whatever she needs," he says. "However, she is also totally insecure. For example, Shannon can't stand being alone. She needs attention twenty-four hours a day. If anything goes wrong or she doesn't get her way about something, she takes a drink, which I hate, or she goes shopping, which I can't really afford right now. I like her twins fine, but I can see that she isn't encouraging them to be normal little boys. They should be out with kids their age playing baseball; instead, they are home with her helping her pick out what she should wear.

"The biggest thing is that with Shannon, nothing is ever easy. Something is always wrong, and she can turn the smallest stuff into a really big deal. Last week my sister and her husband celebrated their tenth anniversary, and they had a party. Shannon went out and bought them a beautiful gift. But at the last minute, Shannon decides that there is something wrong with the dress she is wearing, and she doesn't want to go. It doesn't even occur to her that this is my sister's anniversary and how important it is for me to be there. It took me forty-five minutes to convince her that she looked beautiful. The babysitter helped me, but I could see that she thought we were both crazy. It's like this all the time. Shannon and I went through a lot to get to be together. Why can't we just enjoy it?

"My mother says that there is something really wrong with Shannon, and I'm beginning to think she is right. I love my wife, and I want to do anything I can to help her, but she is one high-maintenance woman. I've taken on a lot here, and I'm getting scared about what I've done. And I don't know what I can do to make it better. With Shannon, it's like normal rules don't apply."

NARCISSISTS PLAY BY THEIR OWN RULES

Narcissism plays havoc with relationships because it involves a belief that one is somehow special and thus above ordinary behavior. If a narcissist is undependable, he may tell himself that he doesn't need to accommodate appropriate expectations; if a narcissist is unfaithful, she has no difficulty convincing herself that she is exempt from ordinary rules. Narcissists tend to cross the line—the line between fair and unfair, the line between self-protective and self-serving, the line between self-aware and self-obsessed, the line between charmingly seductive and manipulatively destructive, and the line between charismatic and egomaniacal. Men and women with toxic narcissistic issues tend to be so involved with their own ups and downs that they cannot realistically see or hear what their partners are doing or saying. They tend to be primarily self-referential—no matter what is happening, it all comes back to "me."

What's the biggest problem with loving a narcissist? Full-blown narcissists view themselves as significantly "more chosen" than others. That means that they often have little or no ability to step into another person's shoes. Their pain, their problems, their happiness, their plans, and their point of view dominate the universe. Narcissists seem to resent doing anything that doesn't somehow serve their self-proclaimed needs—even when their needs appear confusing or even self-destructive.

In our day-to-day dealings with the world, we all encounter various degrees and levels of narcissism. Some people have only a few tolerable traits; others are so self-absorbed that they deserve the label *toxic*. Toxic narcissists take advantage of our good nature and our good intentions; they make us feel exploited and burdened. Many of us work for people with narcissistic issues; some of us have friends whose behavior is arguably narcissistic. These relationships can be demanding and difficult, but typically you still feel as though you have the power to walk away and protect yourself. This sense of power quickly evaporates when you are in love with a narcissist.

HOW NARCISSISTS MAKE YOU FEEL

We can sometimes best identify people with serious narcissistic issues because of the way they make us feel when we are around them. If you are beginning to wonder if the person you love has narcissistic traits, here are some questions to ask yourself:

1. When it comes to nurturing your relationship, are you the one doing most of the work?
2. Do you feel emotionally drained by how hard you have to work to keep your partner happy?
3. Do you often feel that nobody is thinking about how to make you happy?
4. Is the relationship primarily organized around your partner's interests and activities (or lack thereof)?
5. Do you often feel controlled by your partner's moods and ideas?
6. Do other people also find your partner difficult?
7. How often do you cover-up for your partner's moodiness or inappropriate behavior?

8. Are you acutely aware of your partner's selfishness when it comes to dealing with others?

9. Does your partner make unilateral decisions that impact on your safety and well-being?

10. Is your sense of personal safety and security sometimes threatened by something your partner does (such as erratic driving, belligerence, or addictive behavior)?

11. Are you frustrated by your partner's reluctance or even refusal to understand and accept your goodwill and good intentions?

12. Are you often trying to "get back" to where you were at the beginning of the relationship, when your partner seemed to romanticize and idealize you?

Think about these questions. Do they strike a familiar chord when it comes to your relationship with the person you love?

Two

THE "IT'S-ALL-ABOUT-ME" PERSONALITY

"Why does it always have to be about her?"
"Why does he turn everything into a story about himself?"

JOSH, THIRTY-SIX, RECENTLY PROPOSED TO AMELIE, A thirty- two year old woman he has been dating for two years. Although Josh is very much in love with Amelie, he is beginning to recognize that she manipulates every situation so that she becomes the center of attention. Here's a small example: Last week when they went to see a play, Amelie lost her mother's antique pin somewhere in the theater. Amelie convinced the manager to hold the curtain for five minutes while she involved the entire audience in a search for the brooch, which was eventually found in her purse. Josh was embarrassed by the incident; Amelie thought it was funny. Josh used to think that Amelie was adorable and that's why everybody paid attention to her. But as he gets to know Amelie better, Josh can see that she always rearranges situations so she holds center stage. Josh is beginning to think he may be making a big mistake. He wonders, what will his life be like in five or ten years?

He says:

"Amelie can't even go to a play without making sure that she gets as much attention as the cast. Sure, she is also wonderful and loving, but she's making me nuts. She turns everything in her life into a crisis and me into her personal crisis management center. When I first met her, I thought all her little predicaments were cute. Now I don't know what to think. There's always a calamity, a crisis, or a situation. How is it possible for somebody to keep forgetting to put gas in her car? Do you know how many times I've had to drop what I'm doing just to go pick her up? And that's not all. She's totally dependent. Totally. Every time I make a plan for anything, even something as simple as eating a pizza and watching an hour of television, I have to change it because of some emergency in her life. She doesn't care who or what she interrupts to take care of her problems. I'm beginning to think that her emergencies are nothing more than attention-getting devices. What's wrong with her? At first I felt loved and needed; now I just feel abused and taken advantage of. I'm not even sure I want to marry her anymore."

Heather, who is thirty, doesn't have the luxury of wondering whether or not she should marry Michael. They just celebrated their sixth anniversary, and although she is still in love with him, she is also incredibly angry and resentful. Last Saturday afternoon was their four-year-old son's birthday party. Michael planned to play golf in the morning. Heather had pleaded with him to please come home in time to help her with the pre-party arrangements. Not only did he not arrive in time to help, by the time he came home, the party was almost over. Dylan, the birthday boy, was so anxious about his daddy's absence that he spent as much time looking toward the door as he did enjoying his friends. Then, when Michael finally arrived, Dylan greeted him as though he was a returning hero, instead of a selfish father. Heather feels that the only person Michael cares about is Michael. Heather says:

"Michael never thinks about me and what I need; he rarely thinks about what Dylan needs. I assume he was really playing golf on Saturday morning, but I don't know for sure. He could have been hanging out drinking beer with the guys or he could have even been with a woman. It sort of doesn't matter anymore. What does matter is that whatever he wants to do is so much on the top of his mind that he can't even understand that his own little son could be hurting."

TWO PEOPLE = TWO SETS OF NEEDS AND TWO SETS OF PRIORITIES

The above statement is true of every single relationship. It doesn't matter if the relationship exists between two siblings, two platonic friends, two lovers, or two family members. When you go to dinner with a friend, the likelihood always exists that one of you will want pizza while the other craves sushi. When you and your spouse plan a vacation, it is entirely possible that one of you will want to play golf in Palm Springs while the other dreams of the surf at Waikiki. What to do?

In successful relationships, people find ways to compromise and work out differences. Ideally, each person will be able to satisfy some of his/her needs and whims at least part of the time. We can often accommodate and support another person's priorities without doing damage to ourselves. For example, when Fred's wife, Marjorie, says she plans to become a vegetarian and will no longer do any food shopping that includes meat, Fred just shrugs and says, "Whatever." Fred knows that if he wants a hamburger, he can buy it and cook it for himself. However, if Marjorie were to say that she planned to spend their joint savings on an expensive home renovation, Fred would have a different reaction.

When Fred happily watches long-winded pundits on cable news shows, Marjorie smiles indulgently and tiptoes out of the room. However, if he took up gambling or began hanging out in bars all night, Marjorie might well, as they say, go through the roof. As much as Fred and Marjorie love each other, there are limits to their tolerance and understanding. If Marjorie were to push Fred too far, he would begin to feel that his love was being abused. If Fred failed to pay attention to Marjorie's priorities, she would quickly become resentful. Both Fred and Marjorie try to be sensitive to each other's needs, and they want to be treated the same way. Both want to know that they are being "heard." Yes, they both enjoy giving, but they also appreciate receiving.

This is true of all of us. And it's very appropriate. If a relationship is going to work, there has to be—more or less—an even give-and-take. If one person's agenda dominates all the time, the other person will almost inevitably feel burdened and unhappy.

Here's the problem: Some of us feel as though we are in love with people who are incapable of being sensitive to anything except their own needs. Some of us are in primary relationships that appear to be overwhelmingly dominated by the other person's wishes and priorities.

If we were to draw a cartoon of this kind of relationship, one person would have a little bubble coming out of his mouth that reads, "It's all about me!" while the other would be mouthing, "What about me?"

Every romantic relationship presents a source of constant, daunting challenges, perplexing problems, perpetual ups and downs, and very hard work. Relationships are an exhausting business; they ask us to learn and relearn the concepts of compromise, communication, reciprocity, and, every now and then, even sacrifice.

But sometimes we find ourselves in relationships that feel completely lopsided and confusing. One of us shows up with sincere intentions, prepared to do the hard work of relating, but our beloved is showing up with a different agenda—an agenda that screams, "IT'S ALL ABOUT ME!" The all-about-me folks don't seem to want to play by the rules. They don't seem really concerned about our feelings. Our relationships with them aren't organized around things like compromise and reciprocity. Instead, these relationships are organized around the issues, needs, and demands of only one individual.

What these people need and want is somehow always more important than what we need and want.

The all-about-me folks usually present their issues and concerns as though they are of earthshaking importance. They expect us to drop whatever we are doing and make their issues our primary concern. And, often, we do. When we care about somebody, we want to be loving and supportive; when we care about somebody, that person's concerns engage and worry us. But somehow in the process of constantly attending to the other person's "stuff," we start to feel lost. No one is focusing on us. No one is attending to our issues, both large and small. No one is thinking about our priorities. And, in time, we can feel completely obliterated and taken advantage of.

When somebody else's all-about-me demands have you wondering, "But what about *me*?" you have found yourself entangled in the painful dance of the narcissist.

WHAT EXACTLY IS NARCISSISM?

It sounds like a dirty word, doesn't it? But it's not. If we turn to the dictionary for help, we get this information: narcissism = self-love; egocentrism. But we all know that self-love isn't always a bad thing. Haven't we all been told that we need a strong sense of self, that it's important to love ourselves? Aren't we all products and results of a "me"-centered culture? Some have said that narcissism is the plague of our times. Isn't everybody at least a little bit self-involved? So what makes the difference between a reasonable, wholesome, appropriate self-love and toxic narcissism?

The word *narcissism* comes from the ancient Greek myth that tells the story of Narcissus, a beautiful young man who becomes so enamored of his reflected image in a clear pool of water that he is oblivious to everything else. He wants to do nothing but sit and stare at the face that is mirrored back at him. Narcissus is not the only player in this myth. There is also a lovely young nymph named Echo, who is madly and hopelessly in love with Narcissus. Narcissus is the center of Echo's world, and she tries unsuccessfully to get his attention; Echo wants Narcissus to see her and hear her. She adores him and pursues him, but Narcissus runs away. Staring into the pool of water, Narcissus is so absorbed in himself that he is oblivious to Echo. In Narcissus' world view, Echo is obliterated. Unable to look away from his face in the pool for even an instant, Narcissus ultimately dies staring at his wasting reflection.

Hence, narcissism has come to be applied to anyone whose absorption with self outweighs any interest he or she might have in anyone else—even if that self-involvement proves to be self-destructive. A narcissist is someone whose needs are so great that he/she cannot see, hear, or feel the needs of anyone else. This is the picture of narcissism in its most destructive and extreme form.

IS ALL NARCISSISM BAD?

Most psychologists make it clear that there is an admirable and desirable level of healthy adult narcissism, characterized by self-confidence and self-care that we all want. And it is certainly not destructive to sometimes enjoy being the center of attention. There is also the appropriate narcissism of a developing infant. An infant, who is at the center of the mother's universe, naturally perceives the world as an extension of the self. Crying or fussing magically produces food, fresh diapers, cradling, and cuddling. The mother seems to exist solely for the child, creating a cocoon of love and a feeling of specialness. This precious bond between mother and child is a necessary phase of healthy child development. But it is only a phase. As the emotionally healthy infant gets older, this experience of being merged with the mother and at the center of the universe slowly gives way to awareness of separateness. First the infant learns that it is not fused with the mother, but apart. The infant begins to understand the existence of others. As the child continues to grow, it learns more about others: it learns to share, it learns about boundaries, it learns it is not omnipotent. Slowly the infant's view of itself as the center of the universe dissolves into a balance between self and others.

A balance between self and others is an important concept to keep in mind. As adults, if we are to have satisfying relationships, we need to maintain an awareness of the balance between self and others. We need to be able to experience the needs of self as well as the needs of others, and to know that these needs are often very different. We need an ability to care for the self, but we also need a desire to care for others. We need to maintain a sense of perspective regarding the self—an understanding that all human beings are special in their own way, but that none are any more special than others.

DEGREES OF NARCISSISM

It would be wrong to think that the world consists of only two types of people: narcissists and non-narcissists. It's a rare person who doesn't have some degree of narcissism. Narcissism in adults really exists on a continuum, ranging from subtle to wildly toxic and pathological. In some situations, appropriate narcissism can be self-protective and necessary. Isn't it easy for all of us to get caught up inside our own problems and our own point of view? By itself, this is not destructive. But when somebody has no ability, or has completely lost the ability, to experience others as having their own, equally important sets of needs, this person has crossed the line into more serious stuff. Sure, all of us are trying to get our needs met. But when "my needs" become the only needs that count, we are in serious narcissism country. At the far end of the spectrum is the toxic narcissist. This person is totally self-absorbed with almost no capacity for self-awareness or self-knowledge.

If you have ever romantically crossed paths with a full-blown toxic narcissist, you know what an unforgettable, horrific experience it can be; in fact, you probably have your own detail-filled stories of outrageous, infuriating, and obliterating behavior. Even if you have never used the word, you probably have your own personal definition of what it means to know a narcissist. This is a definition that is often filled with anger, anguish, and expletives. It is a definition that you feel in your bones. Typically, you wonder how anyone can be so selfish, self absorbed, and self-involved. How can anybody be so thoughtless and uncaring?

Narcissism is not just a word. It's an experience. It is an all-consuming, confusing, vexing, perplexing, and often an incredibly destructive experience. To the uninitiated, the dictionary definition of narcissism is certainly a helpful starting point. But those of us who have had more than a whiff of the genuine article know that the dictionary doesn't capture any of the real juice; it doesn't capture the essence.

OUR OWN INTEREST IN NARCISSISM

We want to make it clear before we go any further that we are not psychologists. We are writers. Our interest in narcissism evolves from our own life experience. We have both struggled with our own narcissistic issues, and we have both known people who can best be described as toxic narcissists. We have worked for them, been in love with them, and tried to maintain friendships with them. Further, more than ten years ago we wrote two books, *Men Who Can't Love* and *He's Scared, She's Scared*, which introduced the term *commitmentphobia* into the common vernacular of our times. In the process of writing these books and several others, we have interviewed hundreds of men and women about their lives, and we have received more letters, e-mails, and phone calls from people who want to tell us about their romantic experiences than we can possibly count. The stories these men and women recount often revolve around what it means to have a relationship with a narcissistic mate, parent, relative, friend, or boss.

We have heard thousands of stories, of the "how could he/she treat me like that" variety. Inevitably these stories feature a personality whose behavior indicates an off-the-chart sense of entitlement, combined with a stunning lack of empathy. We couldn't help but notice, by the way, that this common denominator—a lack of empathy—dominated so many of the stories we heard about men and women who are toxically commitmentphobic.

Since a lack of meaningful empathy is a predominant characteristic of narcissistic personalities, we began to do more research into the subject. It seemed apparent to us that narcissism and commitmentphobia were often closely linked. We realized that we were intensely interested in the subject and wanted to do a book that looked at narcissism in greater depth, particularly in the ways that impacted our romantic relationships with others. More than twenty years ago, Christopher Lasch wrote a book called *The Culture of Narcissism*. In it, he postulated that we have created a culture of the self-absorbed. Nowhere does this self-absorption become more obvious than in our common struggle to find successful ways to interrelate.

We've written many books together, and we are often asked, "How do you choose your topics?" The truth is that there are few writers who are not connected to their material. It sometimes seems as though it is not so much that we get to choose our topics as that our topics choose us. We have never written a book about sheepherding, and that, no doubt, has a great deal to do with the fact that neither one of us has ever owned sheep.

Something very interesting has happened since we started working on this project. In the beginning our level of enthusiasm was high, buoyed by undercurrents in our own histories that were rising to the surface. The moment we decided to write a book about narcissism, the floodgates of past experience opened and stories came rushing through—about friends, family, neighbors, bosses, colleagues, and a slew of romantic exes, impossible people of all shapes and sizes whose narcissistic issues had disrupted our lives, impinged on our peace of mind, and had sometimes broken our hearts. Yes, yes, yes! Narcissism! The scourge of our lives; the scourge of our times. Before we started the formal interview process for this book, our heads were already filled with stories. But that was only the very beginning—the easiest part of the process.

Once things got underway and we started interviewing people and shaping the material, something very uncomfortable started to happen. We started to see pieces of ourselves in the many stories we were collecting and in the patterns we were trying to establish. It is a terrible thing to be writing a book about "awful behaviors" and "awful people" only to realize that you share some of their characteristics. Julia started to see that her own narcissistic issues may have been what drew her to several men who were much more toxically narcissistic. And Steven began to see how his narcissistic issues were dominating his marriage and diminishing his connection to his wife. And, most importantly, we began to see the ways in which we also had some behaviors that could easily be termed narcissistic. We shudder at the memories of the ways in which we have been self-involved in our dealings with others. We shudder at the memories of the times when we were so wrapped up in our own concerns that we were unable to relate to another person's experience and were unable to hear what others were saying or see what they needed.

Ouch! Nothing hurts more than looking in a mirror and seeing that you embody characteristics of the narcissistic people you are writing about. Let's face it: narcissists may love to look into the mirror, but who wants to look into a mirror that exposes our least desirable side. It brought us both up short. We would have been much happier to have been able to hold onto our lopsided view of narcissism as always being about the other guys. But if we are going to be honest, we have to admit that it wasn't true. It doesn't feel good to have to attach that label to yourself. As we got more involved in the writing of this book, we couldn't help but become aware of the ways in which our world view was solipsistic; we couldn't help but be aware of the times when we were guilty of an "It's all-about-me" point of view. We both wanted to understand and work through our own narcissistic tendencies.

Having said that, we should also repeat that almost everyone has *some* narcissistic issues. Narcissism is a condition of our times, and few of us—with the possible exception of the Dalai Lama and Sister Wendy—are exempt. Understanding narcissism helps us understand ourselves and the world we live in. It helps us improve and strengthen our relationships. It helps us live more honest and open lives.

Three

NARCISSISM, OR OLD-FASHIONED SELFISHNESS?

JUST ABOUT EVERYTHING IN JOHN AND MELANIE'S DATING relationship revolves around what John wants. As a couple, they eat when John is hungry, sleep when John is tired, and turn on the television when John wants entertainment. Melanie is a working mother with a teenage son and a demanding job; John is a freelance photographer with plenty of spare time. Nonetheless, all of John and Melanie's interactions are planned to facilitate John's schedule. Melanie, an independent successful woman, is embarrassed by the retro manner in which she relates to John, but she does it nonetheless because John quickly conveys his annoyance if she behaves any other way.

Because John is perpetually strapped for money, on most of the nights that they see each other Melanie cooks dinner—always a dish that John really loves. One night when John came over, Melanie cooked something John didn't like. As soon as he saw what was on the menu, John said that he wasn't going to stay and would pick up a pizza for himself on the way home. Since then, Melanie makes sure that John's food preferences receive the highest priority. Even as she does this, she complains that John treats her as though she is his mother.

John is trying to save money because he is in heavy credit

card debt. His money difficulties were caused by a "small gambling problem" that took the form of investing heavily into futures trading. John, who says that he will never do this again, acknowledges that he has a gambling problem as well as a rich fantasy life in which he imagines that he is scoring big.

John tells Melanie that she is one in a million, but he usually acts as though she is barely visible. On Saturday night he comes over, bringing his laundry. He eats dinner and then watches television while Melanie washes and folds his underwear, sheets, and towels. He spends the night but leaves early Sunday morning because he has "so many things to do." John may come over for dinner a couple of other times a week, often when there is a ball game because he prefers Melanie's large television set to his own.

Melanie recently discovered that John is investing in the commodities market again; she also suspects that he might be seeing another woman. This is making her feel very confused and resentful. When they first started going out, Melanie was willing to take John's situation into consideration because she thought the relationship would be reciprocal. But that's not how it's turning out. John seems to be oblivious to any of her needs. He is barely civil to her son. He never spends a penny on her, which Melanie didn't mind until she heard rumors about his taking another woman to dinner. When John is confronted with the threat of losing her, he becomes all attentive and caring, but that only lasts for a few days.

Melanie's sister keeps pointing out that John is totally narcissistic. But as far as Melanie is concerned, narcissism sounds like a fancy name for someone who is downright selfish. Is there a difference?

HOW DO WE KNOW WHETHER THE PERSON WE LOVE IS TRULY NARCISSISTIC?

Men and women with serious narcissistic issues have difficulty with social adjustment and regularly exhibit patterns of behavior that are out of sync with what we would consider as appropriate. In a romantic relationship, for example, it is appropriate to expect some quid pro quo. However, men and women who are in love with narcissists are frequently stymied by their partners' refusal (or inability) to conform to normal expectations.

More importantly, narcissists are typically unable or unwilling to change their destructive behavior even though it creates serious upsets in their personal and professional lives. Talk to a narcissist's friends, family, or coworkers; they typically attest to the fact that the narcissists in their lives are unfathomably stubborn about their refusal to compromise or alter hurtful behavior.

Professionals who treat narcissists and their families expect to find certain characteristics. They have even compiled a list. What follows are the nine most common characteristics of the narcissistic personality. Mental health professionals tell us that narcissism is diagnosed by the presence of five or more of the traits on this list. The following criteria are based on or summarized from *The Diagnostic and Statistical Manual of Mental Disorders.*

The Characteristics of a Narcissist

1. An exaggerated or grandiose sense of self-importance that isn't supported by reality.
2. A preoccupation with fantasies of extraordinary success, wealth, power, beauty, and love.
3. A belief that he/she is special and unique and can only be understood by other special people.
4. An intense need for admiration.
5. A sense of entitlement.
6. A tendency to exploit others without guilt or remorse.
7. An absence of meaningful empathy.
8. A tendency to be envious or to assume that he/she is the object of others' envy.
9. An arrogant attitude.

TAKING A DEEPER LOOK AT THESE
NINE DEFINING CHARACTERISTICS

1. An exaggerated or grandiose sense of self-importance that isn't supported by reality.

Explanation: An inflated view of oneself is one of the primary ways narcissists give themselves permission to dominate and control others. A narcissist believes that his/her priorities, interests, opinions, and beliefs have more value and are more important than anyone else's. Not all narcissists fling their grandiosity around the world; some actually appear quite humble or even shy to the outside world, but when they are at home with family, watch out.

EXAMPLE: Most people go to work every day, but when Gregory, the manager of a small supermarket chain, leaves for work, he acts as though he is departing on a "mission." Everything in his home revolves around Gregory having what he calls "a peaceful breakfast" and getting to work on time. His children go so far as to eat their cereal in their rooms in order to keep from disturbing him. His wife waits to use the bathroom or get dressed until Gregory leaves so she won't get in his way. If Gregory is disturbed, he becomes moody; although he actually never loses his temper, he always looks as though he is about to explode. It goes without saying that nobody in Gregory's family breathes normally until he is fully out the door. That's when everybody relaxes and is able to breathe a collective sigh of relief.

Gregory says that his morning routine has to be exactly the way he wants it because of the difficulty of his job. To hear Gregory tell it, nobody in a hundred-mile radius would be able to check their groceries out on supermarket lines if it weren't for him. He is the "only one" who knows how to make things happen at work. Despite his self-proclaimed competence, Gregory hates his job, and when he comes home from work, he heads straight for his computer, where he is trying to drum up interest in a new business he is hoping to start. Not even Gregory's wife can quite understand the nature of this business, but it has something to do with supermarket coupons.

Gregory takes all of his personal and vacation days to work on this coupon sideline. Whenever possible, he makes appointments and takes "business trips" to try to drum up new investors. Gregory's wife is very upset because he has used up all of their savings for this business, as well as borrowed thousands of dollars from his parents, her parents, his brother, and her sister. This has been going on for years, and there has been no realistic outside interest in Gregory's business or his ideas.

Gregory feels that the problem is that he is "ahead of his time." Gregory's wife, who already has a full-time job, is now looking for work on the weekends in an attempt to plug up the holes that Gregory's business has created. His children have learned that their father's need to spend money on travel, clothing that will "make an impression," and computer equipment is "more important" than any of their financial needs; they have learned that all of their father's needs are always treated as though they are more important than their own.

2. A preoccupation with fantasies of extraordinary success, wealth, power, beauty, and love.

Explanation: Narcissists often have active fantasy lives and are rarely satisfied with the merely ordinary, no matter how satisfying or wonderful it may be. This preoccupation with fantasy stops the narcissistic personality from living a real, grounded life.

EXAMPLE: Moira is a talented pianist, but she is having a difficult time making a living. She believes she should be on the concert stage or playing for the Philharmonic and refuses to take any jobs that she considers beneath her. It goes without saying that she won't play weddings or bar mitzvahs. She also refuses to give lessons. Recently she was offered a job playing for a ballet class; this piqued her interest for a short time, but when she went to the interview, she decided that the teacher and the students were mediocre and not up to her standards.

Moira has many of the same kinds of problems in her personal life. She would love to have a relationship with a man, but so far there has been only one man whom she has any interest—a married conductor who is much older. He had no plans to leave his wife, and although he was friendly with Moira and encouraged her career, he never indicated that he wanted to take their relationship any further than a minor flirtation. Moira says that he is the one man she has met who was smart and attractive enough to capture her heart.

Image is very important to Moira. She gravitates toward men and women who are wealthy and successful, and pours her energy into cultivating friendships with people who she believes are gifted, fascinating, or unusual in some way. This isn't really practical for Moira, because she does not have the money or wardrobe to travel in these circles. To have a conversation with Moira is to have a conversation about the important people she knows or would like to know. She doesn't understand why so many of her old friends who lead regular lives can no longer bear talking to her.

3. A belief that he/she is special and unique and can only be understood by other special people.

Explanation: Narcissists are invested in the belief that they are special people. This is typically part and parcel of a coping mechanism that helps them deal with the world. They often define themselves by what they see as their special qualities and let you know about these qualities as soon as you meet them.

EXAMPLE: Barbara presents herself as a spectacularly warm and fuzzy human being; she also believes she is significantly more sensitive than anybody else. She regularly says things like, "I'm sure somebody like you can't understand somebody like me. But I always give more than anybody else. That's just the way I am." When she makes a casserole for the church supper, she manages to tell everybody how good a cook she is and how much time she devotes to caring for others. When she takes her daughter to school, she stops to tell the school guard what a long-suffering, devoted mother she is. When she goes to buy greens at the health-food store, she can't resist telling the owner what an exceptionally good wife she is because she makes sure her husband eats organic salads.

Barbara is convinced that she has suffered more traumas in her life than anyone else and is consequently more sensitive. She has a tendency to become depressed and genuinely believes that no one else has experienced the same level of emotional pain. From her perspective, Barbara believes that nobody could begin to understand what she feels. She can become argumentative when she is challenged. Consequently, the people around her often find themselves catering to her moods. In order to maintain a peaceful environment, Barbara's husband and children completely support Barbara's version of herself. Not that long ago, Barbara had a confrontation at a cash machine when she tried to get in front of somebody because she was "in a hurry." "Just wait your turn, like everybody else," the other woman snapped at her. Barbara got very upset. Barbara's ten-year-old daughter immediately jumped to her mother's defense. "You don't understand," she said to the woman. "My mother is more sensitive than everyone else."

4. An intense need for admiration.

Explanation: Love me, watch me, pay attention to me. Narcissists tend to be self-referential and self-aggrandizing.

EXAMPLE: Sometimes it is downright painful to have a conversation with Celia. She never hears what the other person is saying, and within a few minutes everything is turned into a story about herself. She is the kind of person who, after watching a train wreck from a safe distance, tells friends about it saying, "You won't believe what happened to me today." Celia loves being the center of attention so much that it borders on exhibitionism. She wears clothes that are designed to make people notice her; she has walls of photographs of herself in various situations; she is currently working on a Web site that will feature her opinions on world events; she says her son is successful because of the way she raised him and her daughter is beautiful because "she takes after me." She also flirts with every man, woman, and child she meets.

This need for admiration is behind the self-referential conversations narcissists tend to have. It's all about "my house," "my car," or "my children."

5. A sense of entitlement.

Explanation: Rules, regulations, and expected standards of behavior often infuriate narcissists, who believe they are so unique that they don't need to conform to normal expectations or honor appropriate boundaries. They can be equally distressed by hard work, illness, or injury. When something negative happens to a person with narcissistic issues, the refrain in his/her brain is, "This shouldn't be happening to me! Not to ME!!" If someone puts up a DO NOT ENTER sign up, the narcissist thinks, That doesn't apply to ME!

EXAMPLES:

• If you are Joe's friend, you know that he will never be on time for anything. He is regularly anywhere from an hour to two hours late for all appointments. He says he doesn't understand why it upsets people. Why should he have to conform to such a silly societal expectation?

• Marcus is a superb athlete who has always spent hours every day working out and playing tennis and squash. Recently, he experienced a sports injury that put him in a cast and out of commission. He can't accept what happened. He says, "I honestly believed I lived in a different world, a world where things like this don't happen to you if you're skillful and smart. It just doesn't seem possible that this could happen to ME."

• Karen considers herself an honest and ethical person.

Nonetheless she regularly crosses other people's boundaries to fulfill what she sees as her special needs. She always goes through her boyfriend's wallet when he is taking a shower to try to find out what he is doing when he isn't with her. Through trial and error, she also managed to figure out her twenty-two-year-old daughter's computer password. Now Karen regularly opens up her daughter's files to read her e-mail and personal journals.

• Deidre doesn't believe that the rules the rest of the world follows apply to her. This is true in many areas of her life. For example, she wants to learn how to play the piano, but doesn't understand why she needs to learn to read music. This is pretty much Deidre's attitude toward learning in general. She's so smart that she tends to pick up everything quickly, but then often has only a superficial knowledge, because she doesn't feel that she needs to spend the time to do the work. Deidre parks her car in a parking lot at work every day, but she doesn't think she should have to pay what everybody else pays and she managed to charm an employee into giving her a cut-rate. One day she was driving on the Parkway with friends and there was an accident. Instead of waiting in the traffic jam like everyone else, Deidre worked her car over to the meridian in the center of the highway, straddled it with her automobile, and drove down the center of the road, leaving her passengers in a state of terror, hysteria, and disbelief. After driving with her, one person got a bumper sticker that reads, "I plan to die peacefully in my sleep like my granddaddy, not screaming and shouting like the passengers in his car."

6. A tendency to exploit others without guilt or remorse.

Explanation: Depending upon his/her other personality quirks, a narcissist can induce you to do all the work, take your money, or leave you waiting for hours on street corners in the rain without understanding that this behavior is hurtful and disrespectful.

EXAMPLE: Jenn has trouble understanding her fiancé, Simon, who is also her boss. When Jenn first met him and went to work for him, she thought he was smart, kind, and generally terrific.

As she has learned more about him, her opinion is changing. For example, Simon takes advantage of his friends and his family, particularly his mother and sisters. Jenn knows that Simon manipulates them by making them feel guilty. She has heard him lie to people to get them to do things or pay more than their share of something. Once, when she knew he was lying, she heard him on the phone with one of his clients, saying, "How could you not trust me? That says something about your view of the world."

Jenn realizes that Simon sometimes also uses her. He talks her into working late and on weekends and then makes her feel guilty when she expects to be paid. And she's not the only one. He lies to customers and clients and promises things that he knows he can't deliver, just to get more money. Simon's ex-wife frequently calls the office because he owes her a lot of back child support. The ex-wife told Jenn that it was her money that started Simon's business, a fact Simon conveniently forgot when the business started to succeed. If Simon ever feels guilty about anything he does, he doesn't show that side of his personality.

7. An absence of meaningful empathy.

Explanation: The narcissist has little capacity to step into the shoes of another. His pain, his problems, and his point of view dominate his universe. Perhaps nothing is more reflective of narcissistic behavior than the inability to understand and identify with what others are experiencing. This is particularly true when the person who needs understanding is someone the narcissist is exploiting.

EXAMPLE: Joyce says that the most amazing thing about her wealthy ex-husband is that he never understood how much their children suffered when he left her for another woman and then did his best to give his family as little money as possible. Joyce says, "It was astonishing. He was living in a mansion, and I would be trying to figure out how to find enough money for Sunday supper. My kids were wearing hand-me-downs. I had to take him to court to get him to give the kids money for college, and even then, he gave us as little as he could. He spent more money on lawyers to keep from giving me child support than he did on child support. He never showed us any mercy. The only thing my ex-husband is sensitive to are his own problems. Now he wonders why his son and daughter resent his expectation that they should behave like devoted adult children."

Men and women who love narcissists are often stunned by how little empathy their self-involved partners show. For example:

• "I could accept everything about Bob's infidelity except that he chose to start an affair while I was six months into a difficult pregnancy. He says I wasn't paying enough attention to him, but he either won't or can't relate to many reasons why being pregnant made it all the more painful. I don't think I stopped crying until our daughter was six months old. How could he not understand how I felt?"

• "We have dinner with my wife's family every Sunday, and every week it's the same thing. She and her brothers joke and make fun of everything I do. It's getting real tired. What I don't understand is how she doesn't understand how that makes me feel."

• "I'm killing myself working extra hours, trying to make enough money so Sherri can have the wedding she wants. It's important to her, and I'm happy to do it. The only thing I ask is that she let me sleep late on Sunday mornings, and she won't do it. Can't she see how tired I am?"

8. A tendency to be envious or to assume that he/she is the object of others' envy.

Explanation: It's difficult for narcissists to adjust to a world in which others appear to have "more" or "better." Narcissists frequently fail to acknowledge their envy and instead convert it into contempt. Instead of admiring another person's superior education or greater earning capacity, for example, a narcissist might put a contemptuous spin on it: "Don't you think there is something geeky or nerdy about a person who gets good grades?" or "Anybody who earns that kind of money must have inferior values."

EXAMPLE: Howard, who has an advanced degree from Yale, earns less than his friends. He is surrounded by wealthy people while he is struggling to keep up and pay his bills. He lives in Southern California, and on his way to work every day he drives through Beverly Hills, one of the most expensive neighborhoods in the United States. If anybody is in the car with him, he talks about all the "disgusting excess" he sees. He thinks the people look "stupid"—stupid, rich people with their silly things, their designer pocketbooks and their outrageously expensive cars. He feels nothing but disdain. Howard is in therapy; during one of his sessions, his therapist pointed out to him that he was envious of these people. This was hard for him to accept. He thought all he felt was contempt. He also thought that his friends were envious of him because he was so much smarter. But after talking about it for a few sessions, he realized that envy is the right word. If he had a lot of money, he might not want to spend it the way the people who live in Beverly Hills do, but he is envious of the freedom that money buys.

9. An arrogant attitude.

Explanation: Narcissists are often condescending to those who they think don't meet their "high" standard of intelligence, accomplishment, values, or lifestyle. Believing the "other guy" is inferior helps them bolster and inflate their belief in their own superiority. Being judgmental about others helps them feel good about themselves.

EXAMPLE: Barbie's husband, Todd, is a very successful stockbroker who makes tons of money. Todd can be very charming when he wants to be. However, he is downright condescending and cruel towards Barbie's friends and relatives, who he thinks have cheap taste and lack financial smarts. Todd, who is the "put-down king," goes so far as to refer to these people as "plebes." Barbie doesn't understand why Todd can't realize how much he hurts her by adopting this attitude. Barbie also feels that Todd's behavior is his way of concealing his own feelings of insecurity. It's interesting to note that Barbie is actually very accustomed to this kind of behavior. Her mother put down all of her childhood friends, telling her that they weren't good enough for her. It was very hurtful. As soon as Barbie met somebody she liked, her mother would say something about the child that was as unforgettably funny as it was mean. Although she didn't actually tell Barbie not to play with the kids, a look of disdain would cross her eyes. This made Barbie feel humiliated and as though she had bad judgment. Barbie is very upset that she married somebody who is even more condescending than her mother.

YOU AND THE PEOPLE IN YOUR LIFE

To read the above "list of nine" is quite an overwhelming experience. Remember that experts tell us that five or more of these characteristics should be present before one can be labeled a narcissist.

We ask ourselves: Is my partner a narcissist? Is my best friend a narcissist? Is my boss a narcissist? Am I a narcissist? Is our entire culture one big narcissistic mess? We may know one person with an overwhelming sense of entitlement and another who is outrageously arrogant. We recognize a few obvious traits and a few more subtle tendencies in everyone we know, including ourselves. Most of us are at least a little bit guilty of having narcissistic or selfish propensities. That doesn't make us awful or completely unpleasant to know. It does make us human, with room for improvement.

Most of us will look at the list of narcissistic characteristics and we will have a few "I did that once" experiences and maybe even some "I do that all the time" experiences. Maybe we are a little more selfish than we would like people to think we are. Maybe we can get a little self-obsessed. Maybe we don't always "check in" to see how others are feeling on those days when we're not feeling too great. Maybe we have a hard time experiencing others as equals. Maybe we have a hard time respecting other people's boundaries (maybe we don't even know what that means). Maybe we don't have as much empathy as we wish we had. Many of us will look at the list and we'll recognize not only some of the people we know, but also ourselves. Don't beat yourself up over this. If you can benefit from a tune-up, that's great. Every bit of self-awareness tends to help us move through the world in a more satisfying way. Remember you are reading this book to learn and, first and foremost, how to be more self-protective when dealing with narcissists who are still swinging wild. The world is full of people who still have no capacity to take care of others. These people are not ready to change, and they are unlikely to be interested in doing so. This book isn't for them. It's for *you*. Learn more about narcissism and use this understanding to reshape who you are in the world. It will help you find and build more wholesome, nurturing, and supportive relationships. It will help you become more like the person you want to be.

Four

YOU EXPECT *ME* TO COMPROMISE?

B EING FRIENDS WITH A NARCISSIST MAY TEST THE limits of your saintly tolerance, but you can always let voice mail intercept your calls. Loving a narcissist is a whole different matter. This is someone with whom you share a bed; this is someone you chose to let into your life. This is someone for whom you have intense feelings; this is someone who has the power to thrill you as well as hurt you. This is someone who can break your heart.

It's easy to get confused when you love a narcissist. Sometimes you can't quite put your finger on what is going wrong or why you are so often in a state of high anxiety and distress. *What's going on here*, you wonder. You ask yourself if your reactions and responses are appropriate and justified. It sometimes seems as though your partner is intentionally upsetting you. Is that possible? You wonder if your expectations are askew or if you are letting your partner down because you are failing to be appropriately flexible and supportive or understanding. When you love a narcissist, everything is significantly more difficult than you expect it to be.

Take compromise, for example. Everyone agrees: A good relationship requires compromise. This is a pretty straightforward message. So why do narcissists have such an impossible time understanding it? Why don't they get it? At first glance, compromise seems so simple and pragmatic. You want to go to the movies, and I want to go to the park. Why can't we go to the park first and then see a movie, or see a movie first and then walk through the park? You want to see a horror film; I want to see a French film with subtitles. You want to visit your mother's house for Sunday dinner. What about my mother, who is making lasagna?

When a relationship is new and filled with promise and love, typically even the most narcissistic among us is willing to make some compromises. Then, as time marches forward, everyone has at least a few thoughts like, "Do I really have to have dinner with her birdbrained sister?" or "Why do I have to share my bed with his neurotic cat?" In our current society, in which both partners are likely to have work and career demands, compromise is esssential. In the early stages of a relationship, scheduling can make or break two people's commitment to each other. Most couples discover pretty early on that they have to find ways to compromise about the practical issues of life: handling finances, where to sleep, what kind of a mattress to sleep on, and what kind of food to keep in the refrigerator. Such things may seem boring and inconsequential, but we know of one relationship that went down over two pints of strawberry ice cream, a tiny refrigerator, and the issue of, "Why can't we ever buy the flavor I like?"

Nobody really loves compromise that much. Who doesn't get at least a little bent out of shape by a partner's reluctance to relinquish cherished habits and preferences, even as we feel justified by our own problems with compromise? This is a normal part of the process of working out a successful relationship. Here's the big problem: narcissists really don't want to compromise. They don't want to work at working things out. They want it all to be their way; they believe their way is the right way and the only way. They want their relationships to be structured and organized around their needs and preferences.

"IT'S ALL ORGANIZED AROUND SOMEBODY ELSE'S NEEDS"

In the course of writing this book, we've both remembered too many examples of ways in which we have expected our partners to organize their lives in order to cater to our needs.

Julia says: "I know when I'm working I don't want anybody to disturb me, and I expect my work schedule to take top priority. I always work in the morning, so even when my partner is on vacation, we never make plans for anything in the morning. Even though I have my own office, I expect him to use earphones when he listens to music or watches television, because I'm easily distracted and get annoyed by noise; I expect him to tiptoe around and not to talk to me when I'm working. I guess I never really think about how that makes him feel."

Steven says: "It wasn't until I started thinking about narcissism that I realized how often I 'bulldozed' my wife with my plans. There have been so many times that I've expected her to prioritize my schedule or my needs. Let's take the issue of sleeping, for example. I'm a restless sleeper and like it to be very quiet, so we sleep with the bedroom windows closed and the air conditioner on even though my wife prefers a feeling of open windows and fresh air. I use a sound machine to maintain an even background noise. I sleep great with this thing on, but it actually keeps my wife up; when it's on, she needs to use earplugs. If my wife had her way, she'd read herself to sleep; I want it pitch black, so my wife has given up this pleasure. I'm grateful that my wife goes along with my approach to sleep, but I can see that I'm not very flexible about it."

To some degree, don't we all wish that all aspects of our relationships could be organized around our needs? We would get home from work whenever we wanted, and our partners would be waiting patiently. If we wanted a home-cooked meal, that's what we'd get. If we wanted to go to a restaurant, that's what would happen. If we wanted somebody to wait endlessly in stores while we shopped for items we wanted, that would happen. If we wanted to be alone to watch television, no problem. If we wanted to talk to somebody about anything, anytime and anywhere, a willing and loving partner would be happily available for support and encouragement. Wouldn't that be great? But most of us are smart enough to realize that wish is a fantasy. People with strong narcissistic issues, however, believe that they and their needs are so significantly more "special" than those of their partners that they rarely take anybody else into consideration. They may want to be part of a couple, but they also want to practice unilateral decision making. They may want the advantages of a relationship, but they want it organized around their priorities.

What kind of relationship is this?

Christina, a real-estate agent, is a thirty-eight-year-old single woman; she is trying to build a satisfying relationship with Len, a lighting contractor. Len is a forty-year-old divorced man with a sixteen-year-old daughter. They met at a party given in late September by the local chamber of commerce. For the first month or two, Christina was idyllically happy and Len was totally attentive. During that honeymoon period, Len kept saying that he couldn't believe his luck in meeting someone who was as bright and attractive as she was. Len kept telling Christina, "You're the one—the one I've been waiting for."

As the Thanksgiving holiday approached, Christina was still very upbeat about the relationship. She and Len had made plans to go to the country to visit her sister, Amy, and her husband. Christina had already reported to her sister that she had fallen in love with Len, and she was very excited about having them meet.

Christina's mood was destroyed on Wednesday morning when Len phoned to tell her that he didn't really want to spend

Thanksgiving with her sister. He proposed an alternative plan: that she and Len spend Thanksgiving with his mother.

Christina was so shocked she didn't know what to say. "I thought you told me that you didn't like to spend Thanksgiving with your mother," she replied.

"I don't normally," Len answered. "But I haven't seen much of her lately."

"Is she making dinner? What made you change your mind? I don't understand." Christina was totally confused.

"Are you telling me that I shouldn't spend a major holiday with my mother?" Len asked.

"No, of course not. But we made plans. I just don't understand," Christina repeated herself.

Christina was very upset for herself, but even more so for her sister, who she knew had bought lots of food and was expecting them. "Listen," Len said in a very annoyed tone, "this is the deal. I'm spending Thanksgiving with my mother. You can join us, or you can go to your sister's house. It's up to you."

When Christina first started dating Len, he seemed exceptionally attentive. But as the relationship has progressed, everything is beginning to shift, and Thanksgiving is just one example. Her friends say that she has given Len all her power, but Christina isn't sure how to describe what has happened.

"All I know is that everything has to be done Len's way, and if I make a plan, he will somehow find a way to change it," she says. "This is true of just about everything. Everything. He decides when, where, and what we will eat. He decides what movies we will see and which friends we will visit. He decides what time we go to bed, when we will have sex, and how we will have sex. I sometimes feel he rearranges my plans, just for the sheer hell of it. I'm beginning to feel as though I have no say whatsoever.

"Take last night. for instance. We talked about having dinner at a local restaurant. So when Len picked me up at seven, that's what I expected. Silly me! It turned out that Len had already eaten, without telling me of course, and that he had offered to take his daughter to a junior-high basketball game. When he picked me up, both he and his daughter were in the car. I was famished. When I told him that, he looked annoyed and suggested that maybe I could get something out of the vending machines in the school cafeteria.

"It goes without saying that my dinner was a chocolate bar. Last night with the basketball game is a good example of what happens between us. Each incident, in and of itself, is no big deal. I would be a pretty selfish girlfriend if I wanted to keep my boyfriend from spending time with his daughter, wouldn't I? And if I had said anything to Len, I know that's what he would be thinking. But this is the kind of thing that happens all the time. All the time. Inevitably, every time we make a plan, he calls to say that he has to work late, visit his mother, spend time with his daughter, help his ex-wife with the dog, and so on. There is always a different reason, and every one of them is valid. Any time I say anything, he responds with something like, 'What, you don't want me to make a living?'

"The problem is that this is the way it *always* is. There doesn't ever seem to be a time where our relationship or my needs are given any serious consideration. He wants to do whatever it is he wants to do, and he never wants to compromise at all. And he never thinks about how any of this makes me feel. He doesn't think that I might be hungry, bored, tired, or upset. Two weeks ago, we were on our way to a party, and he decided he wanted to stop at the mall to look at something. I stayed in the car because he said he would only be a minute. I was there for a full forty-five minutes. It was freezing out, and he had taken the keys. I didn't even know where to go look for him. This kind of behavior is a pattern. He never seems to worry about disappointing me or making me feel rejected or stupid. I'm always the one who is adjusting my schedule and doing all the accommodating. It's not fair, and it's making me crazy. I guess I should also mention that Len makes me feel as though I can't complain without risking the relationship. He always tells me he loves me, but he also makes me feel that if I do or say anything he will dump me. It's emotional blackmail, pure and simple.

"The truth is that I'm supposed to wrap my life around his availability, and his availability is incredibly restricted. He doesn't want me to call him at work because he is so busy; he certainly doesn't want me to ever drop in at his office or his house. Yet, he feels free to come and go in my life as he wants. It's all about his needs: he needs to take a nap, he needs to have dinner, he needs to see his kids, etc. Yet, for the most part, my needs are ignored. What kind of a relationship is this?"

Christina is experiencing total frustration. Len treats Christina as though she is an appendage. He won't compromise, and he won't change his behavior. In fact, he doesn't think there is anything wrong with his behavior. From Len's point of view, he is a hardworking guy with a child who is trying to please everybody. All he asks of Christina is that she just be there when he wants her to be there, and not complain. It doesn't even occur to him that she might not enjoy waiting in the cold for him.

About Len, Christina says, "He treats me like I'm his mother." A more accurate description might be that Len has the assumptions of an infant who believes, *somebody will take care of my needs.* This is very much part of the narcissistic construct and goes back to infancy when the child sees his caretaker as an extension of himself, and almost as an appendage. From a baby's perspective, this is an appropriate and healthy point of view. As children develop, however, they ideally reach a point where they can differentiate between themselves and others. There is me, and there is not-me. I have needs and others have needs. Extreme narcissists are stuck in infancy and can only see their own needs.

THE RELATIONSHIP IS ALL ORGANIZED AROUND MY LOVER'S PROBLEMS

In some ways a relationship organized around your partner's problems is even worse than one that is organized around his or her needs. How can you love somebody and not be sensitive to someone's problems, particularly when they are very real?

Elise really does have chronic fatigue; Evan really does have two demanding children; no one can doubt the validity of Paul's money problems; the same is true of Fran's issues with finding and holding a job. But don't we all have real problems?

When you are involved with a narcissist, you quickly discover that only one person's problems really count. What usually happens is that your partner's problems take over YOUR life.

Typically, when we try to help a partner with a problem, we do so because we think that this is part of what it means to be in a relationship. Shouldn't two people who care about each other be supportive and helpful? Of course they should, but most narcissists are incapable of focusing on anyone's difficulties but their own. There is no quid pro quo. Mark, a forty-four-year-old Web designer, told us that as far as his girlfriend was concerned, he had pretty much let go of any expectations that she could be counted on. He says: "Every time Georgina had to take her cat to the vet, I helped her do it; every time she had to be out of town on a business trip, I stayed at her house and emptied litter; every time she was ever sick or pressured or needed help in any way, I pitched right in. Every time she needs me to help her paint her apartment or move her refrigerator, I'm right there. But what about me? Every time I need her to help me, she is either too tired or creates a crisis in her life. Two weeks ago I asked her to help me file some papers because my desk at home is completely out of control. She said she had a cold. A week later I asked again. She said she was so upset about something that happened at work that she felt too depressed to hang out in my apartment. Couldn't we please go out to dinner and a movie instead? She promised that she would do it this week. I know it's never going to happen."

Many narcissists seem to specialize in large problems and carry around a huge amount of baggage, including a history of troubled relationships and addictions of all kinds. When you fall in love with someone like this, it goes without saying that you may find yourself embroiled in a series of heartbreaking ups and downs. Dina, for example, is engaged to Ted, who has two troubled teenagers from an earlier marriage who live with him. Because Dina loves Ted, she wants to build a relationship with his kids, and she wants to make things better for everybody. She is an experienced social worker who believes the children need some positive reinforcement, stability, and a better understanding of boundaries. Since Dina moved in, she has tried to create a more home-like atmosphere; no matter how tired she is, she makes sure dinner is on the table at the same time every night. But Ted isn't cooperating with her plan. He is often late and distracted, and inevitably as soon as he comes home he begins to criticize one child or the other about homework or grades or chores. When Dina tries to discuss childrearing with Ted, he gets annoyed at her, saying "I know how to take care of my kids." Dinner usually ends up being a screaming match between Ted and his kids. Then they all storm off in different directions and Dina is left to clean up. She says, "This is a nightmare, and I think the worst part is that I have no influence on anything that is happening. Ted will not work with me to make things better. Actually, both he and the kids act as though I don't exist. They eat the food I shop for and cook, but that's all. I find myself thinking about this problem day and night. I really want to do something, but nobody will let me.

I'M SO "NICE"—HOW CAN I BE NARCISSISTIC?

A narcissist believes first and foremost that his/her reality, or "story," is the most important one. Some of the most confusing narcissists are those men and women whose impulses are primarily kind, but who are nonetheless terminally self-centered. We think of the story of Marie Antoinette who, when told that the people of France were starving, said, "Let them eat cake." Although she wasn't being mean, she was incapable of seeing beyond her own world.

It can be no less difficult to be involved with a "nice"

narcissist than one who is always angry and mean. Take the case of Heidi and Will and a beautiful spring weekend.

Will really wants to spend Saturday and Sunday with Heidi. Heidi would also like to be with Will. The problem is that if she wants to graduate, she has to finish a dissertation. Because she is determined to do what she has to do, she is home, plugged into her computer and trying to concentrate. So why is Will e-mailing her dozens of little love notes that beg to be answered? In fact, just as Heidi was really beginning to concentrate, Will showed up at her door with flowers, dinner, and wine, saying that after all, she did have to eat.

On the one hand, Heidi is happy that Will loves her and wants to be with her; on the other, she's getting annoyed. She doesn't understand his behavior. Why can't he just be supportive of her goals without superimposing his own? Why can't he see how important it is that she graduate? What's going on here?

Will is so self-absorbed that he can't "hear" Heidi tell him about her appropriate need to prioritize her schoolwork. The loudest "story" in his head revolves around his need for her presence. He wants to maintain his connection with Heidi. This is different than mere selfishness. If Will were primarily selfish, for example, he might think, *Who needs a girlfriend who has to work this weekend? I'll go find somebody else.* Or he might show up at Heidi's door insisting that she make him dinner. This may sound as though we are splitting hairs, but there is a difference.

Somebody can be very narcissistic and very "giving" at the same time. Phoebe, for example, likes to think of herself as a generous and loving person. This is the "story" and view she has of herself. Phoebe overwhelms her boyfriend Larry with attention. It often makes Larry annoyed, and he can't understand why. Here's how it played out last week. Larry came home from work dead-tired; all he wanted to do was collapse. Phoebe, however, greeted him at the door with a big surprise. She had invited several friends over to watch the ball game. She prepared snacks and drinks for everybody. On the surface it looks as though

Phoebe is being giving, but look a little deeper, and we see that Phoebe is going ahead with her story of herself as the "hostess with the mostest," without letting Larry in on it. His needs don't exist. If he were to complain about anything Phoebe does, she would cry and tell him that he's being ungrateful.

NARCISSISTIC TESTING

Narcissists love to test their relationships. Their behavior always seems to be asking at least one of these questions:

- How much do you love me?
- How much can I control you?
- How much can I get away with?
- Will you ever leave me?
- Are you like the others?
- How much can I trust you?
- Do you really love me?

Narcissists do more than think these questions; they act them out in a wide variety of ways. Perhaps one of our biggest mistakes is that we try to answer them. Remember that the narcissist personality has a weak sense of self that needs constant reinforcement and shoring up. What better way to get that reinforcement than by testing the limits to which their partners will go. Consider the following scenario:

Joanna and Thomas have just entered an elegant seafood restaurant located on the bay overlooking the water. The waiter seats them at a good table where they can watch the sunset shimmering on the water. Thomas is taking Joanna out for a birthday dinner, and he is looking forward to a good meal, but Joanna has a slightly different agenda. "Ask him if we can sit over there," she says, pointing to a slightly larger table. Thomas sighs, but does what Joanna asks. He gets up, confers with the maître d', and returns to tell Joanna that the table is reserved for a larger group.

"They're not very helpful, are they?" When Joanna speaks it is much more a statement than a question. Thomas can see that she is becoming moody. The waiter comes over with the menus and to take their drink order. Joanna begins to inspect the menu as though it is a prenuptial agreement. Thomas, who is getting uneasy, wonders what he did wrong. He asks Joanna if she wants some wine. "No," she says. "I'm just going to order water and soda crackers for dinner. There is nothing here I want. You go ahead and order what you like."

"What?" Thomas asks. "Oh, come on," he pleads. "Can't we just have a nice dinner?"

"You can have a nice dinner," Joanna says. "I'm not hungry. I don't mind. You eat. I can just have my water."

The waiter backs off discreetly to let them settle this. A few minutes later, Thomas and Joanna fold up their menus, put their napkins on the table, and leave. Thomas apologizes to the waiter as they are walking out.

Thomas loves Joanna, but he can't understand why she always makes everything so difficult. Why can't anything be easy and relaxed?

Many narcissists can't resist testing the relationship and their partners. It's like a game and it's called "Let's Sabotage the Relationship," or "How Much Can I Get Away With." Narcissists don't feel lovable, and they don't feel loved. They want constant reassurance, and their behavior indicates that they have many "Will You Still Love Me" questions. Here are more:

- Will you still love me if I'm moody all the time?
- Will you still love me if I nag?
- Will you still love me if I flirt with everybody?
- Will you still love me if I sleep with your best friend, your sister, your brother, or your boss?
- Will you still love me if I make excessive demands?
- Will you still love me if I'm so chronically late that there is no guarantee that I will ever show up?
- Will you still love me if I never want to have sex?

- Will you still love me if I never pay for anything?
- Will you still love me if I quit my job and you have to support me?
- Will you still love me if I am always arrogant and mean?
- Will you still love me if I take you totally for granted?

Narcissists often seem to be committed to putting intolerable pressure on their partners and the romantic connection. Testing frequently reflects unconscious issues, but whether conscious or unconscious, it almost always implies that the person doing the testing believes that manipulation is the way to go.

To be in love with someone who tests is to be put through hoops. Some tests are structured for failure. We've known many couples in which one partner constantly pushes the other to the limits of endurance. For example:

• Margo has made Stuart move three times because she hasn't liked any of their rental apartments. She really wants to force him to buy a house, which would burden him with significant financial pressure. Margo was honest enough to tell a friend, "If I don't stop pushing him, one of these days he is going to leave me."

• Adam always changes every plan he and Mai make. She is looking forward to meeting at the zoo at 2 p.m. At one-thirty, just as Mai is about to leave her apartment, the phone rings. It's Adam. He's run into an old friend he hasn't seen in years; he really wants to spend time talking to him. He tells Mai that she is so wonderful that he knows she will understand. He suggests that he will meet her later at her apartment and they can go to a movie she had mentioned wanting to see. By the time he finally arrives, he says he's too tired for a movie.

Some narcissistic testers are specialists in raising the bar; they keep creating more and more difficult situations for their partners to handle. Steve, an extreme example, asked his wife to support him through dental school; then he asked her to support him through medical school. Now, with two medical degrees, he has decided that he doesn't want to do anything that requires patients.

Beth told Sam she would stop nagging if she could only have a baby, even though they couldn't afford one yet. Now, Beth is nagging about buying a house AND having another baby.

The partner of a narcissistic tester often feels that the questions he or she is being asked are:

Do you really love me? Do you love me to the exclusion of your own life?

Five

I'M GOD/I'M GARBAGE

*I*F YOU ARE READING ABOUT NARCISSISM FOR THE FIRST time, you might come away thinking, "Gee, these narcissists must be pretty disgusting, insensitive, and obnoxious people. No reason to let anyone like that into my life." But it's not that simple. Men and women with strong narcissistic issues usually have two conflicting sides to their personalities. Yes, they can appear arrogant, grandiose, and self-serving, but more often than not they are also vulnerable, pained, and unsure of themselves. Often they don't hesitate to express their neediness and insecurity. Every hour of expressed arrogance and entitlement is matched by at least a few dramatic moments of total self-doubt.

Make no mistake about it, narcissistic personalities have inevitably experienced their share of emotional deprivation and hurt. Even when they act as though the world revolves around themselves, from their point of view, emotional pain dominates their internal landscape. They may project arrogance and charisma, but underneath it all they tend to feel unworthy and misunderstood. Most narcissists have this kind of deep contradiction in their personalities; it is often this contradiction that holds our interest and engenders our compassion. More often than not we fall in love with a narcissist because we empathize with their vulnerability. We see that their over-the-top sense of entitlement is an attempt to bolster up a shaky sense of self.

WHICH IS IT: INSECURITY OR MANIPULATION?

Sara, a thirty-six-year-old paralegal, remembers what it was like to fall in love with Robert, a forty-year-old lawyer, a partner in the firm she worked for. She said that they worked together for three months before they became lovers. Sara acknowledges that she was forewarned about Robert. When she first started working at the firm, several people told her about him, saying that he was "manipulative," "a maniac," and "insanely demanding." Their romance started when they worked late one night and ended the evening by going out for something to eat. Sara says that they had no sooner sat down in the restaurant than Robert began confiding in her about his troubled childhood.

"It started by his joking about growing up with his mother, whom he described as the world's greatest serial monogamist. Robert said that his mom denied that she had a sex life; nonetheless, she went from live-in "friend" to live-in "friend." None of them lasted more than two years, and his childhood was dominated by a succession of uncles, at least one of whom had serious problems with alcohol and anger management. Robert said that his mother paid little attention to him or his brothers. The way he put it was, "She was more interested in her own life than she was in her kids."

Robert also told Sara that his mother continued to be very demanding and often inappropriate. He said that she would call regularly to complain about her current boyfriend or ask Robert for financial help. Robert implied that several of the important women in his life had been too much like his mother: they had put their own interests above him and the relationship. Robert told Sara that he had been married once. He said his wife wasn't like his mother in that way, but that she had been boring and incapable of giving him what he needed.

"We sat in that Italian restaurant for close to four hours

while he poured his heart out to me," Sara said, "He leaned in and told me how easy it was to talk to me, and how, although we barely knew each other, he felt an instinctive trust. By the time we finally left the restaurant, to the relief of the poor waiter, I felt as though I knew lots about his life. I didn't even think it was weird that he hadn't asked me much about myself. I thought that we were getting to know each other. I assumed because he was telling me 'everything' about himself that he would want to know 'everything' about me. I fantasized that we would have an open, trusting relationship in which we would always be there for each other. Also, I think it's interesting that I completely disregarded what I had been told by co-workers about Robert's personality. I just assumed that they didn't really know him and that he was demanding because he cared too much and wanted to do the best job for his clients. I honestly thought people were jealous because he was so smart.

"He was so sweet at first. He sounded totally insecure and kept telling me that he couldn't believe that he had met somebody as intelligent and sensitive, and beautiful, as me. He told me how, when he was a kid, everybody made fun of him and how unsure of himself he was with women. Our personal relationship started on that note, with him being tentative and me being supportive and loving. Even though I barely knew him, the way that he had expressed himself to me made me feel as though I wanted to protect him and care for him. I wanted to give him all the love he never had."

Sara says that within weeks of meeting Robert, he had introduced her to everybody in his life, including his demanding mother.

"For about two weeks I was secure. I felt as though I had finally found the relationship I wanted. Of course we had to keep it secret from people in the firm where we worked, but that sort of added to our sense of 'the two of us alone together in the world.' At least that's how it was at the beginning."

Sara said that their relationship quickly entered another

phase, and that soon she began to see for herself why everyone called Robert a maniac.

"We were involved with each other for nine insane months, but our honeymoon period was very short," she explains. "Working with him, I began to see a side of him that I might not have noticed for years if we had only had a personal relationship. I can't even begin to describe the experience. One minute he was self-centered and demanding. The next he was sobbing about how nobody loved him.

"Within the firm he would order people around; he had no mercy. The only reason everyone put up with him was that he was incredibly creative and smart, and he billed so much that he made the firm a ton of money. Also, he was shrewd enough, most of the time, to cozy up to the senior partners.

"No one would ever accuse Robert of being a hunk. In fact, he was downright ugly and kind of overweight. Yet while I was there, beautiful intelligent women were always throwing themselves at his feet. I think these women saw him as this ogre who really had a heart of gold—sort of like the *Beauty and the Beast*. I think they all thought that if they were ever able to reach him, he would totally melt and turn into a sweet, cuddly Pooh bear. Hey, that's what I thought too.

"In the office he would remind everybody all the time how much money he brought in. He took credit for everything good that happened. And, to tell the truth, he may have deserved it, because he is a very talented attorney . . . but he could be very cruel to people. Once one of the younger associates made a mistake. When the associate tried to apologize, Robert called the guy stupid and sniveling. By the time the associate walked away, he was hiding his face so nobody could see it. I looked through my window and saw him get into his car in the parking lot and put his face down on the wheel. I'm sure he was crying.

"Robert made me cry a lot, too. He would lash out at me for no reason. We'd be sitting at home watching television, and he would get cranky and moody. The thing is that when Robert wasn't being abusive he was frequently downright infantile and needy. He hated being alone and said that he felt as though he couldn't take care of basic needs. He had everybody in the office trying to help him furnish his apartment. 'I'm so inept,' he told us. 'I can't even buy dishes. Why do you think I'm the way I am?' He was like a kid crying for attention."

Robert used to tell Sara that he couldn't believe that she really liked him. He said that most women only wanted him for his money or his status. He told her that all of his previous relationships were with women who were much less giving and loving than she was. Statements like that gave her a false sense of security. She says:

"It didn't occur to me that Robert would want somebody else. If he thought I was so loving, wouldn't it make sense that he would want to stay with me? Well, think again. It took him maybe six or seven months before he started cheating on me. It was with a client who was in the process of a complicated divorce. I met her, and I should have figured out that there was something going on between them because she was always trying to do nice things for him. She'd buy him little presents, and once, when we were working late, she sent over a spectacular food delivery from a local deli. When I asked him why she was doing this, he got angry at me. 'What's the matter?' he asked, 'You're going to be jealous of anybody who is ever nice to me?' Then he got this really disgusted look on his face like there was something wrong with me.

"I finally found out what was going on between her and Robert because she called me. She said that she knew that Robert and I were 'close.' She wanted to ask my advice. Robert had told her that I was his 'best friend' but that he didn't find me attractive. She said that it hurt her that he was so insecure and that she was trying to convince him that he was a lovable and worthwhile person. I can't tell you how much it hurt me to hear that Robert didn't find me attractive."

Sara says that something "crazy" happened to her when this woman called. Sara wasn't able to be honest and tell her that she and Robert had a personal relationship. Sara's reasons were complicated. One reason was that she didn't want to get him into trouble with the firm. But a bigger reason was that Sara felt so embarrassed and humiliated that she didn't want anyone to know. After all, she had been warned that Robert didn't care about anybody but Robert. She didn't want to be exposed as a fool. When Sara finally confronted Robert about his affair, he cried and begged her not to tell anybody. He said he really loved Sara, but that he wanted to continue to "explore possibilities" with his divorcing client.

"I quit my job because I didn't think I would be able to see him every day without getting upset," she says. "Fortunately, I got another job right away. I didn't see Robert for almost a year, and then I ran into him. I asked him what happened with his relationship with the divorcing client. He told me that she had broken it off and gone back to her husband. 'See,' he said, 'I told you. Nobody is going to like me for long.'

"Robert was a bunch of contradictions. He was a mean, self-serving jerk, but he was also pathetically needy. He was such a sad mess. I don't know why I found him attractive."

PAINFULLY SAD AND VULNERABLE

This is another trait that should be placed alongside the long list of traits so often present in narcissistic personalities. If you are in love with a narcissist, you know that they don't always show up with an arrogant swagger. More often than not, they seduce their prospective partners by appearing to wear their hearts on their sleeves; often they reveal an unusual level of hurt, sensitivity, or outright vulnerability that touches us deeply. Even if they are obviously self-involved, self-obsessed, or oblivious to the needs of others, frequently these are the people we feel most compelled to protect: "Sure, he seems arrogant, but it's just because he's so insecure . . ." "Sure, she seems overbearing, but it's only because she's so vulnerable inside . . ."

These are some of the common refrains of those who rally around the narcissist. Put a narcissist in front of a magic mirror, and we see a reflection of someone who is emotionally distressed and feeling empty. There is a sad story in there somewhere, and those of us who are drawn to narcissistic personalities manage to find those sad stories. We see the narcissist's pain; we relate to the sadness, and we are disarmed by what we imagine they have experienced. Unfortunately, narcissists can use this pain and sadness to justify everything they do. Nowhere is this more apparent than in romantic relationships.

Marcy, a thirty-nine-year-old woman who has been involved in a long off-and-on again relationship with an extraordinarily self-involved and uncommitted man, put it best:

"People keep telling me to leave David. They say that he is cruel. And that's true. But he's also something else. I would have no difficulty leaving him if he was selfish all the time, but he is also shy, sensitive, and loving. When he thinks he is going to lose me, he falls apart. Sometimes he is like a shy and scared kid. Nobody knows him like I do. Most people don't see the side of him that's scared and dependent."

Marcy's experience is not unique. She identifies with the part of David that is still a traumatized child. The fact is that narcissists are, indeed, often traumatized. And many psychologists believe that much of their difficult behavior is defensive. Men and women who fall in love with blatantly narcissistic partners almost inevitably tell the same kind of story. They were attracted to these men and women not because of arrogance or grandiosity but because within a few hours of their first meetings, these people exposed sides of themselves that were unusually vulnerable and needy; they showed an appealing insecurity.

Here are a few examples:

• "I can't begin to tell you how fragile she seemed when we first met. I thought she needed taking care of. How was I to know that she would turn into a control freak?"

• "He cried and told me that his parents didn't really want

a child and never gave him any attention. He seemed so sad and sweet. Even when he almost put us into bankruptcy, I thought the way he handled money was a way for him to make up for all the love he hadn't received."

• "The first time I met her was at a business meeting at which she was making a presentation. She was totally in charge, and everybody treated her as though she made them nervous. Later, I stayed to talk to her privately, and she was completely different. She was like a scared little kid, worried about how she looked and whether anybody had noticed that her hair was a little messy. I felt as though I had to bolster her confidence and take care of her."

This insecure quality can be very seductive to some of us. We meet the wounded narcissist, and our hearts go out. This person has experienced so much pain that we think he/she will be sympathetic to our emotional needs. This person seems so sensitive that we think that he/she will be sensitive to us as well. The narcissistic personality seems to offer so much promise and potential for a good relationship that we jump right in.

Narcissists are, by definition, injured and wounded. Somewhere, most often in childhood, they lost sight of who they really are. Usually, through no fault of their own, they failed to develop an authentic and durable sense of self. Instead, what they project is a false sense. That's one of the reasons why people with narcissistic issues can be so very concerned with image and how they appear to the world. But, of course, when you see a narcissist in the world, he or she doesn't appear to lack an internal sense of self. What you see is someone whose life seems to be organized around self: self-absorbed, self-obsessed, self-admiring, self-involved, self-serving, self-promoting, self-ish. Every unpleasant *self* word in the vocabulary. This is very confusing. The real picture is this: the narcissist is someone who is consumed by a struggle to maintain an intact façade because of a terrible absence or a core feeling of emptiness. It is a fundamental lack of self that drives the machine we call narcissism.

An Emptiness Inside—Mario's Story

Men and women with narcissistic issues often talk about feeling dead inside. Some describe it as having a sense of an empty center or a feeling of worthlessness that they can't shake, no matter what they do.

It's difficult to believe that Mario, a successful photographer, is insecure about anything. He doesn't appear arrogant, but he certainly seems supremely confident and sure of himself. He's good-looking; he's well educated; he's talented; he has no difficulty meeting women who find him attractive. But to hear him tell it, he can't find a comfortable place in the world.

"There's an emptiness that I feel inside that is terrifying. A couple of weeks ago, on the Fourth of July, I went to the store to get a newspaper. The streets were empty, and it seemed as though all the energy had left the city. I looked around, and I felt just as empty and abandoned as the city. Sometimes I feel so alone that it's horrible. Even when I'm with other people, I feel the terrible, almost cavernous emptiness. Sometimes I feel as though there is a little black cloud inside me.

"I know that a lot of what I feel comes from being abandoned, but I also know that another large part comes from what I feel is a lack of a solid, internal self. I don't feel right being alone with myself because there is not enough 'me' to be alone with.

"I've read everything I can about narcissism because I know that's what I am. That doesn't mean that I'm a bad person or an insensitive person. It means that I can't get away from my discomfort. Therapists talk about narcissists lacking an authentic self and instead creating a false self. I think that until I was in my late twenties, I operated from a very strange place, from a false self that was all bluster and no real substance. I was very aggressive and driven and opinionated. I was animated and entertaining, and, seemingly, full of life. But it was all coming from a place that wasn't real—a place that wasn't hooked up to a 'real' me. In some ways this is like being a caricature of a person. You go out into the world, and you can be very funny, very charming, and very successful with people. You tell yourself that you are relating to people, and that people like you and are impressed by you. When you get home, you continue to puff yourself up and tell yourself how you 'wowed' everybody. You tell yourself how special and wonderful you are. But it's not real. I discovered this when my first major girlfriend left me, and I crashed. I was stunned by how scared and lonely I felt.

"Living without a woman and not knowing what to do with myself gave me the first inkling that there was something seriously wrong. I didn't know how to be alone; I didn't know how to amuse myself by myself. Nothing interested me. I had always been so dependent on being involved with outside activities— work, television, movies, driving my car. I jumped from structured activity to structured activity to avoid the emptiness."

Mario says that one of the most painful things about his life is how difficult it is to find activities that genuinely reflect his own interests.

"I don't even know what interests me. There are times when I get unbelievably angry at my parents for not teaching me more about life—for not teaching me SOMETHING. Anything. Nobody helped or encouraged me to get excited about anything. They squashed any little creative impulses as soon as I expressed them. I might have been interested in art, but they told me that you can't make a living with art. I think I was probably ten at the time. When emptiness creeps up on me, I get angry with them because I feel that I wasn't nurtured in a way that encouraged me to develop a self. I was not supported; I was not exposed to things; I wasn't mentored; I wasn't encouraged to experiment; and creativity was a nonissue.

"I know that I have more of a self than I did five years ago. Being in therapy and learning how to talk to myself and finding healthier impulses has been very helpful. I'm gradually learning that I actually have likes, dislikes, preferences, and even some authentic opinions of my own, not just attitudes that were forced on me by my parents. But I don't have any passions. I'm not talking about obsessions. I mean honest, healthy passion. I don't love things. I don't love to read the comics or do the crossword puzzle or read mysteries or bake cookies or put up dry wall or build loudspeakers or work a lathe.

"I once had a friend who couldn't be at home by herself without the television set being on. My friend couldn't stand the silence. And I remember thinking how awful and sad that was. How empty she must feel, I thought, to need the television set on every moment of the day. But that was when I was living life on overkill and filling my day with endless activity. Work. Errands. Appointments with friends. When my life got quiet, and friends moved away, and I was without a relationship, I realized that I was not very different from this woman. I had the same emptiness. I just had very strong defense mechanisms that had kept me from experiencing it.

"Sometimes I have conversations with people who amaze me: women in their nineties who live alone and feel perfectly content watching the birds and the squirrels; people who live in the country without a neighbor in sight. Just the thought of that scares the hell out of me. The thought of all that 'nothingness'! What would I do?

"Not surprisingly, this lack of an authentic self is something that seems to run in the family. I remember how horrified I was years ago when I would notice that my brother's accent would change with each new roommate. If the roommate came from Atlanta, Georgia, then my brother would sound southern; if the roommate came from Boston, my brother would start sounding like he came from Back Bay. And this didn't happen gradually. The change was fast. I remember thinking, what is happening to him? These days, when I'm more aware of how I take on the coloration of whoever I'm with, I find myself asking, 'What is happening to ME?'

"I'm always searching for people I can connect with, people I can share my life with. I want something from them, but sometimes I'm not even sure what. My sense of self feels so vulnerable that I need constant external reinforcement. I have been told many times, by many different therapists, that I have to learn to mother myself. Learn to soothe myself, comfort myself, entertain myself, and teach myself. I have been told that I'm looking for a mother who doesn't exist because, for whatever reason, my mother didn't exist for me during the crucial time in my infancy when I should have been developing a true self. That's why there is such a hole in me. I have been told that I am the only person who can fill this hole now. I missed getting what I needed the first time, and there is no going back to childhood.

"That thought is terrifying to me. I am terrified that I don't have what it takes to do that. Terrified that I will always feel this way. I still desperately want someone to help fill this hole for me. I still hope that someone will do this for me.

"The most awful thing, of course, is what I do in relationships. Even when I'm with someone I love who loves me back, it still doesn't feel like it's enough. It never feels like it's enough. People who don't know me well would be shocked to hear me express this side of myself. People tend to think of me as overconfident and self-assured. I talk a good game. But anyone who listens to what I'm saying underneath the bravado can pick up the real picture."

If the narcissist seems obsessively focused on externals, it is only because the "internal" is so empty. Inside, there is terror. Inside, there is uncertainty. Inside, there is anguish. And the narcissist spends much of his or her life avoiding that painful reality. When the adult narcissist is successfully functioning in the world (often at some cost to others), all we see is the intensity of "self" activity. But when the defenses of the narcissist fail, the deflation is quick and devastating. Rejection and failure of any kind are crushing to a narcissist, who can go from an arrogant

"I'm the best" attitude to a deflated "I'm the worst" in the blink of an eye. Literally, it can take only a fraction of a second. When the coping mechanisms fail, the narcissist starts free- falling into the abyss of an absent self.

And the interesting thing is that most of us "sense" this about the narcissists we know. We sense this terrible vulnerability, and it seduces us—even when we are incredibly angry or exhausted from their hurtful behavior. There is always something about this person that we just can't help liking. Or loving. We are drawn to the vulnerability; we are willing to put up with a lot because we see something in them, something that needs our help. They can be selfish and impossible and egotistical or egomaniacal. Still, we see their human frailty. We respond because the narcissist is someone in need.

Unfortunately, that need presents a far greater void than any of us can fill. It is not just a need for love or comfort. The narcissist is in need of a childhood, in need of a mommy, in need of a new self. A narcissist is a flailing infant in adult's clothing, desperately trying to avoid meeting his or her own internal truth.

six

WHY ARE NARCISSISTS SO NEEDY?

Why do they demand so much attention?
Why do they so often feel deflated?
Why do they require so much propping and puffing up?

NARCISSISM DEVELOPS AS A CHILD STRUGGLES TO find workable ways to relate to the outside world. In an ideal familial situation, the child's caretakers would be, first and foremost, sensitive to the child's needs and feelings. These ideal caregivers would be aware and supportive of the child's individual and unique abilities and talents. The child would then be able to develop a strong and reliable sense of self. This self would be applauded and supported by generous and unconditional parental love.

Destructive narcissism happens because something goes very wrong during this developmental process. Psychologists tell us that within certain families there is problematic parenting; because of this, the little child who is trying to get a sense of who he/she is in relation to the world is placed under an additional strain. What happens within a narcissistic family structure is that the needs of the child are pushed aside in favor of the needs of one or more of the caretakers. Instead of receiving unconditional love, the child quickly learns that much is expected of him. She is expected to squelch her own sense of self; she is expected to mold herself around parental wishes and expectations. In some families, one or both of the parents may have such strong emotional demands that the child's needs are totally squashed. Some parents have such an overwhelming impulse to be the center of attention that they turn their children into their primary audience; some parents turn their children into extensions of themselves. Some parents are themselves so narcissistically childlike and childish that their children learn quickly to assume parental or caretaking roles.

The child of narcissistic parents had a difficult time. Growing up, he inevitably lived within a family structure where his real needs were inappropriately or inadequately addressed; he rarely felt valued or appreciated for who he was. She grew up feeling that nobody ever heard a word she was saying; she might as well have been speaking a foreign language. He felt alone and misunderstood. She felt squelched and abandoned. He felt as though nobody really cared about him. She felt unloved and unlovable.

A child who is born into this kind of environment must learn survival skills that accommodate the narcissistic parent. This skill almost inevitably requires that the child sacrifices the development of his/her own unique and fundamental sense of self. The child of a narcissistic parent learns at an early age to shape herself to accommodate external demands. This is a child who has lost the connection to his internal voice. It has been paved over. Abandoned. It is in this process that narcissism develops. At the core of the narcissism problem is a comprehensive abandonment of self at the very earliest age. Person, personality, personhood—all are shaped in reaction to the outside world. Authenticity is lost. What typically happens then is that as the child develops, he manages to build a system of defenses and coping mechanisms that conceal this core issue of self. These defenses and coping mechanisms provide the behavior we identify as narcissism; this is the behavior that conceals the core issue of self. In short, narcissists are created by problematic parenting.

"MIRRORING"

One of the essential experiences for positive infant development is "mirroring" from the mother or caregiver. When a baby is born, the caregiver's role is to make the infant's needs primary. The infant is the caregiver's universe and vice versa. During these early interactions, the infant is looking for information to reinforce its sense of who it is and what is it experiencing. The main source of that information is the person who is caring for the infant: what does the infant see when he looks into the caregiver's face; what does he feel when he is held in the caregiver's arms? The caregiver smiles; the infant smiles. The caregiver smiles more; the infant smiles more, reinforcing the original experience. The caregiver is always looking for clues as to what the infant needs: Is that a smile? Is that a frown? Is the baby hungry? What is going on? The caregiver's eyes, face, voice, and hands are giving the infant constant support and reinforcement of the infant's internal experience. The caregiver is attending to the infant, paying attention to its reality, validating its reality, and helping it deal with its reality by talking to it, keeping it comfortable, giving food, and changing diapers.

During this process it is the caregiver who is taking cues from the infant and using those cues to reinforce the infant's experience and understanding of reality. The child is always looking for external validation of its internal state, and this process evolves in more sophisticated ways as the child gets older. The validation an infant or child receives reinforces the child's experience of a "self." In other words, the self does not fully form without validation from the external universe. Mirroring is the process that fuels formation of the self; effective mirroring tells a child that it is safe for her to become her own person.

However, narcissistic parents don't mirror effectively. They are too self-preoccupied; because of this, they are psychologically unable to give themselves over to the world of the infant. Instead of letting the child "become" who the child wants to be, the parents are—from the very beginning—shaping the child (both consciously and unconsciously) to be what and who they feel that child should be. In this way, they practice a kind of selective mirroring. Sometimes the parents are absorbed with their own issues, missing the infant's healthy developmental cues. Sometimes they have decided what kind of person this child will be, and choose to mirror only those things that suit them, shaping the child into their own narcissistic creation instead of allowing the child to evolve from its own internal core.

The self-preoccupied parent causes a twist in the mirroring process: in the absence of an appropriate, effective, and loving mirror, the infant may instead struggle to mirror the parent. The infant does this because it is the only way it feels connected to its caretaker. It is the only way it feels alive. The parent is the infant's universe, and it must maintain a connection with that universe. So the child does what the parent should be doing: the child struggles to pick up cues and clues; it learns to micro-attend the parent's moods; it shapes its existence and its developing self around the parent. The child's authentic, internal impulses are squashed, ignored, and lost as the child struggles to stay alive by doing the job the parent is supposed to be doing.

Learning to mirror the parent is a learned survival tactic, which children do because sometimes it is the only way a child can hold the attention of narcissistic parent, and to lose the attention of the parent is to lose all connection to the universe. But this mirroring is done at the sacrifice of the child's connection to its own authentic impulses, its own internal state, and its own emerging self. This situation occurs when the parent is narcissistic, but it can also occur when the parent is absent or unavailable because of emotional or physical illness. A parent who is going through a depression, for example, is unable to mirror, as is a parent who is dependent on drugs or alcohol. Sometimes, in these instances, the infant or child may try to make the parent better instead of focusing on his or her own healthy impulses.

What this process ultimately creates is a person who has become an expert at paying attention ("attending") to someone else's moods, attitudes, and needs. This is a person who has been forced to shape himself in response to someone else. This is a person who has been forced to abandon her own authentic self. This is a person who walks through the world with a terrible emptiness because he has lost touch with his inner core.

Let's take a simplistic, concrete example to show how this works. Little Susan, who has just turned six, comes home from school with a drawing of a pink tree. Little Susan is so proud of her pink tree that she doesn't even notice the crayon markings that are all over her shirt. But when she shows the drawing to her dad, he notices right away.

"Susan," he says. "Trees aren't pink. They are green. And you have dirt all over that nice T-shirt that your grandmother bought you. She's going to be very angry when she sees it."

In a heartbeat, Susan goes from a happy little girl to one who is feeling bad about herself. She has received at least three very clear messages. Nobody cares about her creative expression or her view of the universe. What really matters and counts is how you look. If she wants to please her father, she'd better think long and hard about what color she paints her trees.

How upset and beaten down a child like Susan becomes from this kind of exchange with a parent is often determined by the level and type of self-involvement the parent exhibits. Perhaps Susan's dad is angry and unkind as well as self-involved. He could add a meaner phrase like, "I can't stand looking at you in that dirty shirt." He could then totally ignore Susan, leaving her feeling very hurt and also very angry. She could begin to seriously question her sense of self. She could be left with angry impulses that are difficult for a small child to handle. This is how narcissistic rage and the process of learning to disconnect from that rage begins to form.

But let's assume for a moment that Susan's dad doesn't want to be that unkind. The self-referential communication with his daughter could continue further in a different way. Instead of nurturing Susan's talent or paying attention to her interests, her father could turn the entire exchange into a story about himself.

"Susan," he could say. "Trees aren't that important anyway. Let me show you what I was doing today. Let me show you what I was doing on the computer. After that we can watch the ball game together because that really interests me. In the meantime, let me tell you a story about something that happened to me when I was a little boy. Your grandmother still has some pictures I drew when I was a little boy. I'll bet she'll show them to you if you ask."

From this exchange, Susan gets another message: if she wants to have a relationship with her dad, she'd better learn to listen to his stories, share his values, and be willing to talk about what interests him. She'd better be willing to let him take center stage.

We can see from this that although Susan's dad isn't able to relate to Susan as a separate and creative entity, he is willing to include her in his world when it suits him. Susan's dad is also very charming, and when he reaches out and shares his interests with Susan, she feels as though she belongs; she feels connected. It doesn't take long for Susan to understand that if she wants to experience that sense of connection, her own interests are going to have to be buried, and she will be spending a lot of time paying attention to her dad's stories.

Obviously there is nothing wrong with a parent sharing his life and enthusiasms with a child. In and of itself, this is a good thing. It becomes a problem when the parent does it to the exclusion of any other kind of relating; it becomes a problem when the parent ignores the child's talents and abilities; it becomes a problem when the parent expects to be nurtured and supported by the child instead of the other way around.

Let's think a bit more about how Susan's exchange with her father could play out and impact on her life. Remember Susan's dad is not a mean person; he's just self-involved and ignorant about children. If Susan starts acknowledging her anger at her father for his offhanded rejection of her pink tree, she will probably end up being upset with herself. After all, her father shares his ball game with her. How can she be angry with him? So even if little Susan realizes that she's not getting the life support she needs, she buries her anger, her disappointment, and her hurt. She pastes on a smile and goes off to watch the ball game with her father. She may even think something along the lines of "Isn't daddy wonderful?" or "Daddy seems pleased when I learn the names of the ballplayers. I have to do this more often."

Despite his attempts to build a relationship with his daughter, Susan's father is still a classic narcissist in that no matter how the story starts, it always ends up being about him.

Of course, some parents are much more hostile and destructive than Susan's father. We talked to one man who said that when he was seven years old, he drew a picture in school for his mom for Mother's Day. When he ran home all excited and gave it to her, she said, "This is what you give your mother for Mother's Day! You call this a present?"

CHILDREN WITH A SHAKY SENSE OF SELF

Children who have grown up with self-absorbed and self-referential caretakers typically fail to develop an authentic sense of self. To compensate for this deficit, what they develop instead are coping mechanisms that will help them deal with their unhappiness and distress. This is where a rich fantasy life that promotes a false sense of self comes into play. In their heads these children begin to run away to different places where they feel better. Their fantasies allow them to be strong, talented, powerful, and, most important, special. In their fantasies, they assume center stage. In this way, they begin to inhabit a world that isn't totally real; in this way they develop a "false self" that keeps them safe and protected from moody, unreliable, or destructive parenting. This is how the "someday when I'm rich and powerful" stories start. This is how the children of narcissists protect themselves, and this is how a new generation of narcissists develops.

To some degree, we all have a false sense of self—a self that we put forward like a suit of armor to defend and ward off life's traumas and attacks. Some of us do it automatically when we go off to work every day: we put on the clothing we wear like uniforms and pick up our satchels, briefcases, and toolboxes; when we do, we also put on at least a little bit of false self. This is the face we wear when we face the general public. This is the person we present to the world, no matter how crummy or tired we may feel.

Creating armor and defense systems is an all too human characteristic. Narcissists carry this to the nth degree. They create fantasies about themselves for themselves as well as others, and they cover their stories in armor so strong and unbreakable that it resembles material that might be used by NASA. They have a false sense of self that is frozen in place. It is permanently installed. Underneath it, however, they may feel as though they are perpetuating a fraud. They often complain of the If I'm So Successful, Why Do I Feel Like Such a Fake syndrome. Nonetheless, they continue to foster the same kind of life; they continue to create stories about themselves. They need to do this in order to feel okay about themselves. They need to do this in order to compensate for the authentic self that failed to receive the support it needed.

Not surprisingly, this combination of self-confident armoring and low self-esteem can create a visible contraction in the language and behavior of the narcissist. One minute we are dealing with the controlling, self-serving adult, the next we are relating to the insecure child whose sense of self needs excessive amounts of support and shoring up.

TAKE CARE OF YOURSELF!!!

We think this is a good time to stop for a moment and remind readers that they shouldn't be so sympathetic that they fail to be self-protective. Anyone who is in love with a narcissist knows how easy it is to be moved by a narcissist's essential sense of loss. We make our biggest mistakes when we think that somehow our good intentions are going to be enough to help our loved one overcome all the deprivation he or she feels. Some years back, Julia dated a man who told her up front that he had some narcissistic issues. She says:

"He was in his late thirties, but I was still in my mid-twenties, and not all that sophisticated about this kind of psychological problem. I had no idea what narcissism meant. He gave me several books about the subject, which I dutifully read. I also listened to him talk at some length about his original narcissistic wound and his internal feelings of narcissism and loss. It sounded very sad, and I have to admit that all the emotional intensity he expressed made him appear interesting.

"When he talked about the level of pain, discomfort, and emptiness he experienced in daily life, it made me more sensitive to him in general. I remember thinking that I would do everything in my power to make sure that I never caused him any more sadness. I wanted to be the one to make him feel better. Now, of course, I recognize how my own issues with narcissism fed these thoughts. I would be 'the one' who would heal his emotional traumas. In return, I expected that he would be my 'true love.' In reality, it was a roller coaster ride of a relationship that left me feeling pained and betrayed.

"One night we were at a party given by a woman I knew. My boyfriend and I were standing talking to her when he turned to me and said something along the lines of 'Honey, could you make me a sandwich.' Sure, I told him. I went over to the buffet and carefully put together a plate for him with a sandwich and salads and stuff and brought it back to him. Our hostess excused herself as he took the plate from me. He looked at me and there were tears in his eyes.

"'You're the first person in my life who I could comfortably ask to make me a sandwich. If I had asked my ex-wife, she would have told me to make my own damn sandwich. No woman has ever given me what you have.'

"His teary eyes held mine, and I was overwhelmed by what he appeared to be feeling and what I felt in return.

"That was the kind of moment on which I based a belief that he truly loved me. Our relationship eventually ended because he was remarkably unfaithful, and nothing I did was enough to chase away his demons.

"Years later, long after our relationship had ended, I had lunch with the woman who had given that party. 'There is something I've always wanted to tell you,' the woman said to me, 'but I felt too guilty.'

"'Oh?' I said.

"'You remember Jack, that guy you used to go out with?' she asked.

"'Of course. What about him?' I answered.

"'I did something I'm totally ashamed of,' she told me. 'I had a brief affair with him.'

"'When?' I asked.

"'Do you remember that party I gave?'

"'Yes,' I nodded.

"'I still remember his asking you to make him a sandwich. While you were gone, he told me that he was totally attracted to me and asked if we could get together. I'm so sorry,' she said. 'He told me that your relationship was mostly platonic and that it was almost over. I don't know why I believed him. I guess I was flattered. He was such a player, but I wasn't smart enough to figure out what was happening. There is no excuse for what I did, and I've always felt guilty.'"

When she heard this story, Julia says that her jaw literally dropped in disbelief.

Seven

THE STORIES THEY TELL

"Noel and I met on a blind date. Within minutes of his sitting down next to me in a coffeehouse, he began telling me about himself. I was completely fascinated by his stories about his life and his upbringing. He made everything from his parents to his personal choices and conflicts seem incredibly intense and exciting. For a long time, I saw everything from his perspective. That, of course, changed with time."

—Darcie, thirty-eight, describing how she met her ex-husband

W HEN WE FIRST MEET THEM, NARCISSISTS CAN appear quite fascinating. More often than not, they like to tell stories about themselves. They tell their stories to the people they meet, and they also tell them to themselves. It's fair to say that the typical narcissist is fantasy-driven. It's also fair to say that the more grandiose the narcissist, the more grandiose the fantasies. This doesn't mean that all narcissists are outright liars (although some certainly are); it does mean that they are masters at "spinning" reality and the true facts of their lives.

Once again: the narcissist feels as though he is missing a reliable and trustworthy sense of self. He compensates for his loss by using his fantasies to create another self—a false self.

A false self is something we construct when we believe our real selves need protection and we don't want to reveal our feelings to humanity at large. We create a false story, and that's what we put forward for people to see. We all do this, some of us more often than others. We feel sad, so we tell jokes. We feel guilty, so we pass on the blame, as in, "I wouldn't have dropped the orange juice on the kitchen floor if you had screwed the top on right." We feel vulnerable, so we act belligerent. We feel inadequate, so we get expensive haircuts, put on designer suits, and concentrate on looking competent. The jokes, the blaming of others, the tough façade, and the expensive clothing are all forms of personal armoring.

We all sometimes feel as though we need some armor to help us face the outside world. The biggest problem with armoring occurs when we begin to believe in it as opposed to believing in ourselves. That's when we lose touch with our sadness and think of ourselves as jokesters; that's when we forget that we hold some culpability for our actions and focus on blaming others; that's when we use our clothing and our attitude to conceal our insecurities—even from ourselves.

Under certain conditions, the armoring provided by our stories is self-protective, but it can also end up being harmful because it keeps us from understanding and handling our emotional concerns. That's what happens with narcissists. Instead of facing and working on their underlying emotional issues, narcissists focus instead on keeping their armor firmly frozen in place. They put their energy into maintaining their false fronts and their false stories. This is how they survive their own internal injuries. Let's take Dick, for example. Dick grew up as a lonely child, with workaholic and very successful parents—dermatologists—who essentially ignored him. As an adult, Dick, who is about to finish his medical residency, has created a story that presents his family as though it is an altruistic dynasty. Dick has convinced himself that the primary reason why his parents were neglectful was that they were devoted to the greater good of humanity. All of Dick's stories are essentially true. Dick's parents did work one day a month in a clinic with minimal pay. But when Dick talks about his parents, he leaves out the fact that most of their practice was a lucrative one that involved acne and rich kids; he focuses almost entirely on the do-good elements. The story he tells makes him feel better about himself.

Narcissistic behavior emerges from the stories narcissists tell themselves about themselves. Most narcissists have developed and created an interesting story. The most toxic narcissists tend to have the most dramatic and intriguing stories. These stories allow narcissists to delude both themselves and others.

Struggling to maintain their stories, narcissists are constantly bouncing between two sets of feelings. One set can be described as "puffed up." These puffed up feelings revolve around a sense of being entitled, and, let's face it, at least a little bit better than anybody else. This is the false and inflated self. This is *the* story. Dick's puffed-up story, for example, is that he is the "doctor son" of "doctor parents," and that, like his parents, he has a calling to care for others.

The second set of feelings can be described as "deflated." Deflated feelings speak to an almost all-pervasive sense of shame and worthlessness. When a narcissist feels deflated, he may feel depressed and think of himself as boring, unattractive, and less interesting than others. She may describe herself as foolish or stupid, or lacking in self-esteem. Dick's deflated feelings revolve around his sense of shame over not being like other kids. Why *were* his parents missing for all his childhood events? Why *did* they fail to attend PTA meetings and school bake sales? What *did* he do wrong to keep them from even attending his birthday parties?

FEEDING THE FALSE SELF

It's no fun walking around feeling deflated. So what to do? In order to stay puffed up, narcissists need to make sure that they or someone else is regularly reinforcing or feeding the false self.

That's one of the ways that they use the people in their lives, particularly their romantic partners. They need to have people and situations that make them feel important.

It's important to keep in mind that few narcissists have the skills or the inclination to sign on for any long-term programs that might enable them to make real, deep change. Remember the Greek myth of Narcissus staring into the pool. Narcissism is about externals and the way things look on the surface. Keeping it superficial, narcissists typically want some kind of instant gratification that will change the way they feel, even if it fails to address the real problem. Because of their surface approach, when narcissists attempt to change the way they feel, it often exacerbates or adds to the original problem. Here's a simplistic, but valid, example. Stan can't pay his bills and worries about being and looking poor. He feels so bad about himself and his economic condition that he goes out and buys an expensive new car. For a few days, at least, he will look and feel rich; for a few days, at least, he will tell himself a story that revolves around how successful he looks in that car. That will make him feel better. Buying that expensive new car is how Stan will puff himself up and feed his false self. Ultimately, of course, it will make him feel even crummier about himself and his financial condition, and so the cycle continues.

A Puffed-Up Story Substitutes For a Real Life and a Real Self

Mary, a thirty-six-year-old social worker with a nine-to-five job, regularly complains about her boyfriend's need to be the life of the party. "I don't understand him," she says. "Last week we were at a party. It was midnight and a work night. The temperature outside was three below zero. We both had to go to work the next day. Almost everybody else had gone home. But Seth was sitting and talking to two women, telling them his many stories—all of which I have heard a dozen times. And he wanted to stay there. He looked annoyed when I tried to get him to leave. Why didn't he want to come home and curl up in our cozy bed? He claims he loves me. Why did he want to stay there? What did these women have to do with our life? It's not even that I'm jealous. I just don't understand why he needed to do this."

Several of the people we've talked to have had similar complaints about their narcissist partners. They have a tough time comprehending why narcissists need—or even want—so much attention and reinforcement from the outside world. One man described his wife as an "attention junkie." He said, "I hate it that it's so easy for somebody else to grab my wife's attention. It feels as though her family—me and the kids—aren't enough for her."

Bradley, a forty-three-year-old man who has been in long-term therapy for narcissistic issues, told us about some of the misguided steps he took to get attention, puff himself up, and bolster his own faltering sense of self.

"I remember when I was in my twenties going through a period where I had the feeling that I was a very uninteresting person. I didn't think there was anything interesting or exceptional about me at all. I believed that I had an empty upbringing, basically watching television every night in a boring, neighborhood in a boring small town. Then I went to a boring college and started grad school. It all felt so empty, which I realize now had to do with my own sense of self.

"When I first met people, and they asked me about myself, I would tell them that I was in grad school getting a business degree, but I could almost see them yawning. A future working in a corporation loomed in front of me; to make myself feel better, I decided to take some time off from school and travel through Italy and the south of France. I felt that if I had an adventure, then at least I would have something to talk about. So I took a year off and moved to Europe. For a year I lived a life that most people only dream about. Once I did that, I had a story to tell. It was a strange year, because part of the time I was totally exhilarated, but for the other part I was ready to throw in the towel and run home because I was so intensely lonely. I kept telling myself, You have to do this. You have to acquire more character.' I was determined to acquire experience, determined to become a more interesting person, so I stuck it out. Because I didn't really know how to entertain myself by myself, I relied on finding people I could hang out with.

"By the time my year was up and I went home, I really was a changed person. I had seen incredible things and had some extraordinary moments. And now I was filled with stories. Now, in my head, I thought of myself as the adventurer. When I met people, I didn't tell them about being in grad school; I told them about Mediterranean beaches and charming little restaurants in the south of France. I told them about beautiful, glamorous French women and high rollers in Monte Carlo. When I told these stories, even I felt like an interesting person.

"But it didn't take much for my veneer to disappear. Lack of an appreciative audience—that's all it took. If all of my stories meant nothing to someone, they meant nothing to me. Like the women I was dating. If a woman found my stories uninteresting, I was uninteresting. I was immediately deflated. And if it was a woman I cared about, I was devastated. When that happened, I immediately began to think about finding new adventures and new stories. In my life, when all else failed, I used travel as a means of creating a false self. The self I wanted to be was a sophisticated world traveler.

"But, ultimately, it didn't work. Because if somebody didn't pay attention to my interesting stories, I felt ten times worse. Now that I had a more interesting past and had become such an interesting person, I really felt that I should be admired. This problem continues to this day. With all that I've done in my life, and I've actually accomplished a great deal, if someone I meet acts disinterested in me, it reduces me to zero. I feel this way in every aspect of my life. When people are paying attention to me personally or professionally, I feel high. Like I could conquer the world. But if that interest is withdrawn, I'm deflated—worse than before. It's as though there is nothing inside that keeps me from crashing. I am completely dependent on external validation. I have a hard time understanding this sometimes. If someone who I think should be paying attention to me isn't doing it, I feel hollow and worthless."

Bradley used travel to create a false self and overcome his feelings of unworthiness. While it may not have given Bradley what he wanted, travel in and of itself is not a destructive pastime. Many narcissists use far more toxic means to conceal their insecurity and puff themselves up. Let's look at some of them.

Idealizing and Devaluing Others

When it comes to dealing with others, narcissists tend to swing between the two unrealistic extremes of idealized overestimation and complete devaluation. Often they have parents who dealt with them in extremes as in "This is the best, most talented child in the world," or "This is the most ungrateful, impossible child in the world." Looking at the world from this polarized point of view is something many narcissists begin to do in childhood.

Sometimes idealization is directly connected to a child's pattern of creating a protective view of their parents. A cruel and narcissistic mother, for example, may elevate her behavior; she may look her child in the eye and say, "I'm such a good mother and a good person, I don't know how I ended up with such a bad child." A child in this circumstance often goes along with a "story" that supports parental idealization because it may be easier to accept and embrace than the reality of a rejecting mom or dad. Further, children of narcissistic parents are often lonely and may create idealized fantasies to assuage their feelings of unhappiness. These childhood patterns form the basis of a lifetime of fantasy and the extremes of idealization and devaluing.

As adults, narcissists continue to have a hard time with reality and seeing things as they really are. When it comes to love and romance they often form unrealistic (and frequently hidden) crushes. When they meet a new person, they may immediately overestimate and idealize this person as being "totally good and wonderful." Later, they may view the same person as completely "bad and negative." They prefer to view the world in extremes and see only those parts of others that support their extreme all bad/all good view. Many narcissists bolster their self-esteem by forming immediate and often dramatic attachments to people whom they believe (however momentarily) exemplify characteristics that they admire. For example:

• Cheryl drives her friends and family crazy by "falling in love" with a new person every month. She always starts out with incredible enthusiasm. Then, just as inexplicably, she "turns off." When this happens, she doesn't even want to share this information with the former love object. She asks people to lie for her and say she moved or can't come to the phone.

• Martin has a rocky work history. What usually happens is that when Martin gets a new job, he falls in love with it. Everything is great; the people are great; the work is great; the environment is great. Within weeks or months, he begins to notice things that aren't so great, and he decides that he can't "take it." As soon as he finds one problem, he begins picking away until he notices dozens of problems. All the things that he loved about his work situation, he begins to hate. So he starts looking for a new job.

When the narcissist is on an upward swing of idealizing people or situations, he will usually feel good because he has formed such a "positive" connection. But when things don't go exactly as he had hoped, he may well turn completely negative.

This pattern of idealizing and devaluing others and self is one of the underpinnings of the narcissistic personality.

Making Themselves Feel Better by Making Somebody Else Look Bad

Some narcissists seem to get special pleasure out of being hurtful and putting others on the defensive. This quality allows them to maintain a story that tells them that they are better than others.

This behavior, which can be particularly difficult on their nearest and dearest, can take many forms. Some examples include:

IT'S ALWAYS THE OTHER GUY'S FAULT

Narcissists are quick to assign blame and find fault; as anyone who has ever loved a narcissist knows, it's difficult for them to "own" their own behavior. For example, after six years of marriage, Lois asked Leon for a divorce because she was tired of living like a single parent. Lois felt as if she carried the full responsibility of their two children and the house. On weeknights, after Leon left his office, he stopped in at a local bar and restaurant, where he played pool and hung out until after ten and sometimes later. On more than one occasion he went home with a woman from the bar. He played golf every Saturday and Sunday. Those rare times when Leon was actually home, he was either sleeping or eating chips and glued to the sports channel. If Lois asked him to help with anything around the house, he got angry. Now that they are separated, Leon says that he and Lois weren't getting along because she had turned into a "nag" and was "no fun."

"CAN'T YOU EVER DO ANYTHING RIGHT?"

Is there anything more painful than a romantic partner who is consistently critical? Most of us hoped to fall in love with someone we could trust to be sensitive and accepting. Toxic narcissists want to be unconditionally accepted while they dish out criticism and contempt. They do this so they won't have to look at their own failing; they do this in order to maintain their armor of superiority.

TURNING THE OTHER PERSON'S SUCCESS INTO FAILURE

Narcissists love to demean other people's accomplishments:

- "The only reason Ed got that promotion is because his wife is friendly with the owner's sister."
- "You think Gwen is so great because she does so much volunteer work. Let me tell you, the only reason she does it is so she can feel good about herself."

- "It's not that Luke is such a great skier; it's that he has great equipment."

Narcissists are easily threatened when others are successful and are rarely able to appropriately compliment others. They simply don't like to relinquish center stage.

JUDGING AND PUTTING OTHERS DOWN

Most narcissists are overtly as well as covertly judgmental. They are always talking about other people's failings, never their own. By being contemptuous of others and putting them down, they puff themselves up. "Look at how that man treats his wife," the unfaithful narcissist says. "Can you imagine?"

That, by the way, does not mean that you can count on their actions to genuinely reflect their judgmental words. Perhaps nothing is more confusing than discovering that your narcissistic loved one is regularly engaging in some behavior about which he has been critical. For example:

—Jonathan is shocked to learn that his girlfriend has a drinking problem. That's because she has so often spoken scornfully of women who drink too much.

—Cynthia has just found out that her boyfriend has refused to pay child support to his ex-wife and may go to jail. She is incredibly surprised, because he has said so many negative things about deadbeat dads.

It goes without saying that narcissists are way less judgmental about themselves, and they quickly find ways to eradicate any guilt they might feel over any of their actions. Hey, they prefer to make others feel guilty.

Making Themselves Feel Better by Acting As Though They Feel Bad

Kelly describes her ex-husband, Sloan, as a toxic narcissist who has broken the heart of every woman he has ever known. She says that Sloan's main stories often revolved around how guilty he felt over some of his past behavior in relationships. When she met him, he told her a story about how he disliked men who hurt women. He told her how upset he felt over how badly he treated the women he had known before her, including his former wife.

Kelly says, "Sloan cried up a storm. He sobbed and said he didn't know how I would ever be able to love somebody who had been as insensitive to women as he had been in the past. He swore that things would be different with me. I certainly believed his sincerity, what with the tears and all."

A few years later, while they were still together, Kelly discovered that Sloan was involved in a long-term affair with somebody else. As luck would have it, Sloan's girlfriend discovered it at the same time and phoned Kelly. The two women sat up half the night piecing together all the stories they had been told. They discovered that they had both had identical conversations with Sloan in which he talked about how guilty he felt about the women he had treated badly. The only difference was that when Sloan cried in front of this new woman, he included Kelly in the list of women he had hurt.

Using Addictions to Maintain Their Stories

"I drink the most when I feel bad about myself."

"I first took prescription drugs for physical pain, but I became addicted to them because of emotional pain. I just felt bad about my life, and they helped me feel good."

Given what we know about the "false self," it's easy to understand why alcohol and drugs can be so appealing to so many people with narcissistic issues. What better way to conceal and deny the authentic self? What better way to deny and avoid pain? What better way to run from one's own unhappiness? What better way to create and maintain a false story for the world to see?

The guy sitting at the bar telling tall stories about himself and his conquests is a familiar caricature. But that doesn't make the caricature any less true. Tom, a forty-eight-year-old advertising manager, hasn't had a drink in five years, but he remembers vividly what felt like to get drunk every night. He also remembers how alcohol stoked his grandiosity to the point where he felt almost omnipotent.

"I admit that I used alcohol to make myself feel better about myself," he says. "I was one of those drunks who always had a million stories to tell. When I'm drunk, I'm pretty funny. I also loved to argue with people, and when I was drunk I would argue with anybody. That's because when I was tanked, I felt like a king. I felt like the smartest know-it-all on the planet. I loved those feelings. It made me 'high' in the truest sense of the word. I felt as if I could do anything and nobody could touch me. None of it was real, of course. Then I would wake up and feel like a total failure with a hangover. I spent years that way. I would still be drinking if I could, but I ended up with three ex-wives (all married when I was drunk and divorced when I was sober) and cirrhosis of the liver (which nearly killed me). Otherwise, I would still be drinking, because I loved the way it made me feel."

Alcohol and drugs are but two of many addictions that are directly connected to narcissistic behavior. Others include:

—**Shopaholics:** Spending and shopping are common ways of allowing oneself to live in a fantasy world. People have various explanations for their addiction to spending. Some simply say, "But the only time I feel good is when I shop." This behavior almost always comes down to a desire to inflate oneself with grandiose dreams.

—**Sexual addiction:** This is yet another effective way to feel attractive as well as powerful and thus bolster an uncertain view of self. Narcissists often use their sexual attractiveness and seductive skills as a highly effective way of manipulating others and feeling larger than life.

It's Fun When People Fight over <u>Me</u>

A favorite story that a narcissist likes to encourage is that he/she is the most important person in the room. Here is one surefire way for narcissists to hold the center of attention: keep setting up triangulated situations that make your partner feel left out and jealous. Men and women who are regularly unfaithful or even unusually flirtatious and seductive typically have at least a few unresolved narcissistic issues.

An intimate relationship is something that happens between two people. Add a third, and it becomes a triangle. We can guarantee that, at that point, everything will change. In schoolyards across America, teenagers typically learn the expression, "Two's company; three's a crowd!" Narcissists frequently add that third person, and when they do it, it is a surefire way to become the center of attention.

Triangles can be created even when there is no overt sexual infidelity. Here's a modern-day example. Jake spends much time on his computer answering e-mail and forwarding jokes and information he thinks might interest his friends. He keeps many new and old connections alive in this way. Last week, he and his girlfriend, Gayle, had an argument over this. She has always found it upsetting that every time he sends her a joke or a letter, there is a good chance that it is going to a couple of dozen other people, most of them women. Almost every time she receives e-mail from Jake, she sees the screen name of his ex-wife and his ex-girlfriend, along with a host of other feminine sounding e-mail addresses she doesn't recognize. Lilybabe7400, SuzieQ???, Fredreika33Wow! are some notable examples. She wonders: who are these women, and what do they mean to him? He insists that they are just friends, but what, she asks, does this mean?

The argument between Gayle and Jake became more complicated recently for the following reason: Gayle had received an e-mail from a close friend, talking about a movie the friend had just seen. Gayle sent this to Jake because she thought the two of them might enjoy the movie together. Jake, in turn, labeled the e-mail "Movie Review" and forwarded it to everyone on his large list. It made Gayle feel that there was no place for her just to be with Jake and Jake alone. It made her feel that Jake is always setting her up to compete for his attention. She also feels that Jake violated an intimate trust by forwarding a personal letter without talking to her first. Jake says that if Gayle didn't want him to forward her friend's letter, she shouldn't have sent it to him. As far as he's concerned, he was just being inclusive and friendly. Another observer might see the obvious confusion in Jake's boundary structure and realize that his electronic communications can be viewed as a subtle way of violating his intimate connection to his girlfriend.

When we think of triangulated relationships, we typically assume that they always have a sexual component. This doesn't have to be true. Tony, for example, always seems to find ways to pit his wife against his mother, or vice-versa. Sometimes, if his mother doesn't want to play this game, he turns to his sister. At Christmas dinner he almost always manages to get three women—his mother, his sister, and his wife—competing for the right to wait on him.

Debra has a similar dynamic with her husband, Mac, and her father, whom she consults about many, if not all, of the decisions in her life. Mac and Debra have been married two years and already Mac feels displaced. He says, "She talks to her father about everything, and before she talks to me." Mac says that he gets the impression that Debra "gets off" on having him compete with her father. "I think it makes her feel more important somehow."

Using Image to Puff Up the False Self

As traumatized individuals who lack a strong stabilizing sense of self, narcissists focus on image and externals to help compensate for that inner void. Like Narcissus himself, their eyes are fixated on the image and easily fall into a mind set where they believe that everyone is staring at them. It is a rare narcissist who isn't going to have some skewed image issues. Many are excessively concerned with one or more of the following:

- Do I look attractive?
- Do I look wealthy?
- Do I look successful?
- Do I look unique and special?
- Do I look enviable?
- Do I look different from everybody else?

Many a narcissist honestly believes that if she is able to create and maintain the image she desires, she will be able to have the life she wants; many a narcissist honestly believes that he will be judged solely on his image.

Does this have anything to do with relationships? You bet it does! If you enter a narcissist's world, chances are how you look is going to take on incredible significance. Do you look attractive? Do you look wealthy? Do you look successful? Do you look unique and special? In short, do you present the image that the narcissist wants in his/her life? Now let's extend this to everything about you: Does your home environment present the right image? Do your children, clothes, pets, car, and gear present the image the narcissist wants? Do they help the narcissist maintain his/her stories of greatness?

We remember talking to a woman who was complaining about her narcissistic husband. Picture this scene: Sally, who is nine months' pregnant, enters the hospital bending over, clutching her large tummy. She is in pain, and her water has just broken. Her husband is by her side; his arm around her.

"Try to stand up a little straighter, honey," he is saying. "People are staring at us. As soon as we get in the hospital, you'll need a paper towel to clean your shoes."

The narcissist may appreciate and pay lip service to your

inner beauty, intelligence, and ethics. But when push comes to shove, what this person will tend to value most is all external.

Bad Behavior and Worse Stories

- "How could anybody who says that he loves me leave me to handle all these problems with a new baby *and* the new house while he takes off to Hawaii to go on a business junket with his friends?"
- "How could he plan a fishing vacation for the two of us without telling me when, he knows that I'm allergic to mosquitos?"
- "Why would someone who says she loves you go and sleep with your best friend?"
- "How could someone who says he loves you and wants to spend the rest of his life with you maintain a secret relationship with another person?"
- "Why would someone who says she loves you tell you so many lies?"
- "How could he get so involved in listening to his music that he forgot to feed the baby?"

How could she? Why would he? Men and women in love with toxic narcissists often spend a lot of time asking themselves these questions.

Men and women who love narcissists often articulate a sense of disbelief; they are always looking for answers to the questions of "How could he do this to me?" and "How could she treat me like this?" The answer is that narcissists are inevitably most concerned with maintaining their fantasies and stories about their own importance. This is what allows them to feel puffed up and good about themselves. To that end, the narcissist is like a junkie who will rob his family in order to get high. Narcissists will use whatever they can to maintain their fantasies.

If a narcissist is in pursuit of a new sexual conquest, for example, his/her momentary feelings of being powerful and attractive may completely outweigh any sense of commitment or integrity. If a narcissist is receiving positive attention from an admiring audience, he or she might consider that more important than a crying baby. If a narcissist is getting a sense of unlimited possibilities from an out-of-control spending pattern, that sensation will take priority.

No matter how peculiar a romantic partner's behavior may appear to you, there is something in it that is temporarily helping that person feel puffed up and inflated. And, for the moment, at least, that feeling is more important than any plans or promises he/she may have made with you.

The only people who can understand narcissists are other narcissists. The rest of us have to acknowledge the difficulties involved in trying to relate to someone who is a) lacking in genuine empathy and b) without an authentic center.

Part 2

HARDWIRED TO FIND
NARCISSISTIC PARTNERS

Eight

ALL MY GREAT LOVES HAVE BEEN SELFISH

W HEN BONNIE'S FRIENDS ASK HER WHY SHE puts up with her narcissistic boyfriend's behavior, Bonnie always has the same answer: "I love him." Her friends invariably then articulate the same follow-up questions; "Why? What is there about him to love?" Bonnie always shrugs, as if she can't explain what keeps her attached to a person who is so hurtful.

Anyone who has ever been in love with a narcissistic and emotionally abusive partner knows what it is to defend one's romantic choices. Friends ask, "Why do you want to be with him?" or "Why do you put up with so much sh-- from her?" There are no good answers. How can anyone describe a feeling of bonding and connection so intense that it feels as though your narcissistic partner is welded to your soul and has been with you since birth—or even before.

But why does it happen?

Here's a sad bit of news. Most of us who fall in love with narcissists do so because we are no strangers to the narcissistic pattern and have some narcissistic issues of our own. Typically we are the products of a narcissistic family structure, which means one or both of our parents exhibited narcissistic behavior.

That doesn't necessarily indicate that our caretakers were mean or vicious or completely disinterested in their children. It simply means that they had narcissistic issues.

Because of this, we are accustomed to organizing our lives, our priorities, and our time around another person's wants and needs. Our families and our immediate environment prepared us to fall in love with partners who were self-absorbed and self-involved. Coming from families with narcissistic issues, we don't find narcissistic values or attitudes unusual. We grew up with people who encouraged idealization and fantasies. We have probably been conditioned to go along with another person's agenda and don't think it's that strange or unusual to be asked to do so. It may even feel familiar and comfortable. "Maybe the reason I love Harry (or Mary) so much is that he/she reminds me of my father (mother)." Or "I really understand Harry (or Mary) because his/her father (or mother) reminds me of my own."

If we want to know why we fall in love with selfish and self-involved partners, we have to go back to our original loves. We need to think about the cast of characters that includes our parents, grandparents, caretakers, and siblings. That's where we began our journey, and that's where we can find the information to help us change the nature of our relationships.

If we were to talk about a classic example of someone growing up with a narcissistic parent and then moving on to narcissistic mates, we would probably look to Cathy.

Cathy, who is now forty-two, has a history that is filled with upsetting relationships with highly self-involved and selfish men. By anybody's standards, Cathy, a slim woman with shiny, shoulder-length blond hair and flashing hazel eyes, is extremely pretty. Cathy has a large number of friends who find her both funny and kind; she also has a great many talents and makes her living in television broadcasting.

Cathy wants very much to find a partner with whom she can build a lasting and loving relationship. To that end, she has spent several years in therapy; this has helped her begin to understand some of the relationship dynamics that both attract and repel her.

CATHY'S STORY

"Both of my parents were very self-involved, so I guess it's fair to say that I have always loved narcissists. My mother was self-involved, but she wasn't unkind. When I was growing up, my mother was depressed most of the time and wasn't very available as a parent. Thinking about it, I kind of forgive her because my father made her so unhappy. But I find it very difficult to come to terms with my father. Part of me is really angry at him all the time; another part is in total denial of the way he is. I keep expecting him to change and be more accepting and loving, but I don't think it's going to happen. The main thing about my father is that not only did he always want everything his own way, he was also mean. Everything always was and is about his following his impulses.

"Growing up, I remember that my mother didn't like to get up in the morning, so my sister and I would get dressed and come downstairs to make ourselves breakfast. As soon as we came into the kitchen, my father would move to another room so he didn't have to be bothered by us. Then, he was supposed to drive us to school, but just as we were ready to leave, he always remembered some little chore—like balancing his checkbook. We would stand there waiting with our coats on until he finished. He made us late all the time. I can't imagine why he did this. He seemed incapable of taking our priorities into account even when they were reasonable ones, like being on time for school. I don't know if he was totally unaware of how difficult this made it for us in terms of our teachers, or if he was just sadistic. The one thing I remember most about my childhood is that we always had to cater to my father's moods."

Cathy says that despite her father's need to have everything his way, she still adored him and wanted to please him.

"He was my daddy. He would teach us things and take us to museums. We would follow him around and listen to him lecturing; he liked that role. But he always had to be the center of attention. I remember once creating a crossword puzzle from scratch. I designed the whole thing, with the black squares and the white squares. When it was finished, I was very proud of it. I showed it to my father, who of course changed the whole thing and then finished it himself. My mother got furious at him. I would write a poem, and he would rewrite it so it came out the way he wanted. My mother said he couldn't stop himself—everything had to be his way.

"My father was a dentist, and he took care of all of our teeth. I think it's very telling that he used Novocain for other people, but never for his own family. My mother would cry and plead with him to use some painkiller, but my father thought it was less of hassle not to give the shot. He had some rationalization about why this was a good thing, so we all listened to him. It wasn't even a question. I got used to the pain and never thought it was weird until I grew up and had Novocain for the first time. He would perform dental work on all of us while we were in total pain. This was particularly true of my mother, who would cry, but her tears didn't seem to make a dent in how he did things. I know I'm repeating myself when I say that everything had to be totally his way, but that was just the way it was."

Cathy said that her father hated it if anybody else was the center of attention; he wouldn't move off center stage, even for his own children. Cathy told us that this was true not only with Cathy also with her sister.

"My older sister had a lot of talent as an artist. When she was in junior high, all of her teachers encouraged her to take more classes. My mother finally enrolled her in oil painting classes at the museum. The first day in class, she turned around and there was my father. Instead of just appreciating her work, or taking classes someplace else, my father went to her class and competed with her the whole time."

As an adult, Cathy now realizes that her mother also wasn't very successful or effective in coping with her marriage or her children.

"I think she was just depressed and out of it most of the time. One of my favorite stories about my mother is that she would sometimes forget to pick us up. Once it happened when my sister and I were coming home from a school trip. We all piled out into the parking lot, and the other kids' parents were pretty much already there. The buses and everybody took off, including the teachers. I guess it didn't occur to anybody to do a final check. Fortunately one teacher looked back, and she came and waited with us, expecting my mother to pull up any minute. But nothing happened. We kept telling the teacher that my mother had forgotten, but she didn't believe us."

A major theme in Cathy's relationship with her father is how he treated her and the rest of the family financially.

"My father, who made a very comfortable living, always complained about money. It was nonstop. By the time I was a freshman in college, my mother couldn't bear one more minute of the marriage. She was so tired of dealing with him that she just walked away and didn't ask for much; she was worn out and knew how difficult it was to get him to part with his money. She moved into a small studio apartment. On the summer between my freshman and sophomore year in college, I guess I expected I would be able to come home to my old room in the house in which my father continued to live. I had no place else to be. But as I prepared to come home for the summer, my father told me I couldn't do that because he had rented out my room. He said he needed money. It simply never occurred to him that I was still a kid. He always acted like I should be taking care of him rather than the other way around. He sat me down and told me how I had to be more sensitive to his financial concerns. By the time he was finished talking to me, he practically had me convinced that I should go out and support him. My father likes the part of being a parent where his children pay attention to him; he hates the part where he is supposed to take care of anybody else.

"When I went to college, I had scholarships and two and sometimes three jobs working on campus so my father didn't have to pay any of my tuition. Between the scholarships and work, I made enough for tuition. My father came to the college financial office with me and very efficiently arranged it that the money from my jobs all went directly to my school for tuition so none of it passed through my hands. What this meant is that I still had to sometimes ask my father for walking-around money. I can't even describe how much he resented giving me money and how bad he made me feel. I would do without just about every-thing rather than ask him. If he had to give me even the smallest amount, he would complain and make me feel terrible. It didn't matter how many jobs I had or how hard I worked, by the way, my father still made me feel like I wasn't doing enough.

"Soon after the divorce, my father married his second wife. Then he sat my sister and me down and explained that he didn't want us to think that our house was our home any more because he wanted to be able to walk around naked with his new wife. It's interesting that these days when I avoid going to his house for family functions or anything, he complains that I have no sense of family."

Cathy describes her father as always being self-referential. No matter what she tries to discuss with him, it always has to refer back to him.

"If I tell him that something good happened to me, he says, 'That reminds me of the time that I . . .' Then he tells me of some incident in his life. He does the same thing if I tell him something bad happened to me. He has no capacity to pay attention to anything that anyone else says. It simply doesn't interest him. When he pays attention to me, even now, it is almost always negative attention. He always loves to tell me all the things that I do wrong or that I should be doing something else. When I graduated from college, he came to the ceremony and told me how I had taken all the wrong courses and gotten the wrong degree.

"The other thing about my father is that he is always whining and crying that his children are not nice to him. He always complains about how I treat him. He tells me that I was always a difficult child. One day he asked me, 'Why do you think you cried so much as a baby? You wouldn't stop.' He said, 'I used to pick you up and shake you, and you would still keep crying.' He didn't even think that was a strange thing to say."

Cathy said that she knew her father was selfish and self-centered, but it didn't occur to her that the way she related to him would have such a drastic effect on her adult relationships. On a conscious level, she certainly didn't want to fall in love with somebody who was like her father and, in fact, always expected that she would fall in love and live happily ever after with someone who was totally different from the man she called dad.

"What I didn't think about was how I was primed to respond to selfish men. I don't ever seem to notice it until it's too late. I got married when I was in my twenties, and I guess I expected a fairy-tale marriage. What I got instead was Brent, a man who paid absolutely no attention to me. It was as though I didn't exist. Brent lived in his own world. He was like my father in that most of the attention he paid to me was destructive."

Cathy said that she felt that Brent loved her as much as he was capable of loving someone, but he didn't know how to show it. He would also find fault with everything about her, from the way she dressed to the way she talked.

"He would yell at me all the time. More than once he shoved me up against a wall because of something I did. Once I remember that I stood up to him and raised my voice. He took his hand, covered my mouth, and said, 'Just shut up.' When I got upset about how he treated me, he told me that being a husband wasn't one of his priorities."

Cathy says that her ex-husband always had a real sense of entitlement.

"One of the things I remember about Brent was that he felt that he didn't have to follow normal rules. That included small stuff like not leaving the refrigerator door open or turning off the stove when he was finished using it, as well as bigger stuff, like not going through STOP signs. He even ran up my credit cards and I had to pay them off. When I complained about anything, he told me that I was a nag and to get off his case. Probably the biggest problem was that he drank too much. Brent didn't see his drinking as a problem. He thought the biggest problem was that I complained about his drinking."

By the time Cathy and Brent broke up, Cathy said that she felt totally depressed, vulnerable, and alone. She immediately began looking for a new partner.

"I was so hurt by Brent's lack of interest that I was a total pushover for anyone who was even a little bit nice to me. In the last few years I've gone out with a variety of men, all of whom were primarily selfish and narcissistic. With every man I meet, I seem to still be replaying my relationship with my father. I realize that with all of them, my attitude has been: If I do this, will you love me? If I do that, will you love me? If I twist myself into a thousand different shapes and do everything you want, will you love me? It's disgusting."

Cathy says that one of the things that she is really beginning to notice is that many of the men she's found attractive have showed relatively little interest in her life.

"It's my father all over again. One of the most telling things about my father is how he reacted to me on September 11, 2001. I live in New York City, and I knew people who worked in the World Trade Center. In fact, it was not inconceivable that I could have been there. By mid-afternoon on that awful, awful day, I had spoken to many friends and co-workers, all of whom were receiving phone calls from parents and family members who were anxious to know that they were okay. I guess I needed to reach out and touch someone so I phoned my father, who lives in another state.

"It was a knee-jerk reaction to the emotions of the moment. I really didn't expect my father to be any different than he ever is. He answered the phone and without even asking me about the city or the event, he immediately began to tell me about his day: he had a dental appointment; he was reading a book."

"Did you hear what happened here?" I asked him.

"Yes, of course."

"Well, weren't you concerned? Were you going to call?" I was dumbfounded by his lack of interest in anything except what he was doing.

"Of course I would call," he said to me. "I was planning to call everyone tonight when our rates go down."

Cathy says that now when she meets a new man, one of the things she is very much on the lookout for is his capacity to think about anyone but himself. She says that she has to learn to be more conscious about what it is that she is attracted to and why.

"I think I've finally realized that I have to fix myself before I can recognize and respond to a man who doesn't remind me of my father. Right now, that's what I'm trying to do, because I want to have a good relationship."

DEREK'S STORY

Derek says that he really likes women and is jealous of some of his male friends, who have ongoing relationships with supportive women. Derek feels that he has been very loving and sensitive with the women in his life, so he doesn't understand why he has never found anybody. Derek has his own consulting business and is very stable professionally and financially. His relationship history, however, has been primarily frenetic and difficult for him to understand. When we asked him about his history with narcissistic women, here's what said:

"If by narcissistic you mean self-involved women, let's just say that I've dated my share. I have been involved with so many crazy women that right now I'm not even dating. It feels safer that way. Let me tell you about my last girl friend, Sandi. She launched a career as a "cabaret singer" when she was in her late thirties. The first time I went to see her perform, I don't know what I expected because I had never heard her sing.

"She made a lot of the people she knew come to see her, so there were almost twenty of us—friends, cousins, one of her aunts, a couple of gay guys she hangs out with. When we talked together at the table before she started her act, we discovered that none of us had a clue that she thought she was a singer. It was a Wednesday night, and the place was almost empty— which, it turns, out was a good thing. She was so bad, it was embarrassing. Sandi is a terrific salesperson, but even so, I don't know how she talked the club owner into giving her a shot. It was humiliating. After the show, none of us knew what to say, but she acted like she thought she was terrific. 'I know I need a little work,' she told me, 'but I definitely think I'm on the right track. I've finally found my niche in life.'

"I met Sandi because she was a volunteer for a local political candidate; she was with him at a house party I attended. She acted like she was some kind of representative of his. She seemed very lively, intelligent, and well spoken. I think I was impressed that the candidate thought enough of her to let her speak for him. It turns out that she had sort of invited herself along; he didn't have clue one who she was, and I guess didn't know how to shut her up.

"I was with her for almost a year, and by the end of that time I had kind of figured out that she was some kind of major bullshit artist who always made herself seem more important than she was. She had dozens of stories about her life, and I doubt if half of them were true. She said she had a boyfriend who died from a drunk driver, and she was still mourning him, but when I met members of her family, nobody had ever heard of him or knew what I was talking about. I overlooked a lot of that stuff, but then she started trying to take over my life. She wanted to own me, and not in a good way. I came home one day and discovered her in my apartment. She had called my brother and told him she was planning a surprise party for me and talked him into giving her my key. What she was doing was going through my drawers and cabinets and reorganizing them. She couldn't understand why I got angry."

Derek says that he realizes that he can't really blame Sandi for the demise of the relationship.

"Like I said, I seem to be attracted to crazy women. And I know that it started with my mom. I'm in my mid-forties, and my mother still has the power to wipe me out. My mother has two sisters and a brother, and nobody else in the family is like her. I don't know where she came from.

"Growing up, my mother wasn't like any other mother on the block. She didn't think normal rules applied to her. Everybody made excuses for her. When I was real young, my father's mother lived with us and took care of us. I attribute any normalcy that I have to that time in my life. My grandmother was very nurturing; she did all the cooking, cleaning, and childcare when she was with us. But it wasn't good enough for my mother, who complained and put her down all the time. Everybody always tiptoed around my mother. Everybody! My father, her mother, her brother, her sisters. Nobody ever had the guts to make my mother do anything. It was always easier to just let her have her way.

"My mother didn't even want me or my brother to go to school. She said we were too smart for that. You have to understand that this was years before anybody heard of homeschooling. I should also add that we were not being homeschooled. The authorities were always at the door, and when we did go to school, we were understandably behind everybody else in the class. My mother is very proud that she is different from everybody else, so she made sure that her kids were different. If all the kids in the neighborhood were wearing jeans, she'd insist we wear white shirts and sport pants. If the other kids were playing baseball, she'd tell us that baseball was for boys who were inferior, and she didn't want us to be inferior. She didn't even let us learn to swim because she read an article about bacteria, and from that day forward she decided the water was too dangerous and filled with germs.

"My mother had some grandiose ideas about what she should have been; she always talks about the career she could have had if she didn't get married and have children. She was never very maternal in terms of being normally protective, and we always had to take care of her. If anybody ever complimented me for anything, she always chimed right in saying that it was because of something *she* taught me."

Derek said that while he was growing up, he remembers his mother complaining constantly. She said the house wasn't big enough; their father didn't make enough money; the neighborhood wasn't intellectual enough. She never let up. Derek doesn't remember his father fighting with her, but when he was about ten, his father announced that he couldn't take it any more and left.

"I think he wanted to take us with him, but she wouldn't allow it. In some ways with him out of the picture, life at home got better, because at least we didn't have to hear them fighting. But things certainly didn't get more normal. My mother always courted disaster and set up situations for things to go wrong, and then when they did, she cried poor me, and how could this happen to me, and everybody is against me. Almost every month the electricity and phone were turned off because my mother didn't pay the bill, even when she had the money. I don't know why she thought she was exempt from paying. Then, instead of dealing with the situation, she would go to her sister's house so she could complain about how unfair everybody was to her. She would be there having a nice dinner and complaining while my brother and I were home alone sitting in the dark without a phone. Now I realize that this was abnormal behavior, but at the time it seemed perfectly natural that my mother should be having somebody make her dinner, while we were alone. And my aunt always sent food home for us, but it was pretty late by the time we got it.

"When I turned seventeen and left home, my younger brother went to live with my father, and I think in some ways he had a better adolescence than I did. He also had more distance from our mother, which I think was good for him.

"I was only nineteen when I got married for the first time; Dorrie was twenty-four—an older woman with a two-year-old little girl. My mother didn't shut up about this; she said Dorrie was manipulative and she only married me because she couldn't get anyone better. She said Dorrie was using me to get her daughter's father jealous. It turns out my mother was right. But her carrying on didn't improve the situation.

"The scary thing is that my mother had bad things to say about every woman I've ever known, and she is always right. My brother won't have anything to do with my mother because he says that she is determined to break up his marriage. I've always gotten the brunt of my mother. The worst thing, of course, is that so many of the women I've been involved with are just as crazy and self-referential as my mother.

"I would really like to meet a normal woman and have a normal life. But I seem to be drawn to neurotic women. Like my mother, most of them have trouble holding normal jobs.

"I've thought about this a lot, and I think the primary connection between my mother and the women in my life is that they are all looking for attention and they are all a little bit broken. For reasons I don't understand, I'm attracted to this kind of woman. I think I can take care of them.

"These women seem to know how to involve me from day one—often they have life situations that make me feel that I will be needed and valued. I have a friend who tells me that there is something wrong because I have never really gotten angry at my mother or any of the other women I've known. I always understand them and feel sympathy for them. Just like I do with my mother.

"If you met my mother, you would like her. She's very charming, and she talks a blue streak. She's funny and smart.

She dresses like a normal person and talks a good game, but she's incapable of ever thinking of another human being. My mother's brother, her sister, my father, my brother, and I support my mother. We give her as much as we can, but she complains about all of us—often to each other. She is always telling us things about each other and trying to create trouble."

Derek says that as much as he tries to give his mother, she is still primarily selfish, childlike, undependable, and, yes, manipulative. He says that he has come to accept it, but that sometimes it still hurts.

"Let me tell you what my mother is like. Last year I had a terrible flu. I was so sick. All I wanted was some ginger ale and Pepto Bismol, so I called my mother and asked her if she could buy some and just put it in front of my door. I didn't even ask her to come in because I know she is phobic about germs. My mother is in her mid-sixties, but she is a very healthy woman. She plays tennis and does yoga. She's very fit. I don't feel guilty about asking her to drive a couple of miles. At first my mother said, yes, she would do that. Then a couple of hours later, while I'm still waiting, she calls me up and says she has been thinking about my request, and she's decided that one of the reasons I'm still single is that I am too dependent on her, so she doesn't think it's a good idea for her to bring me the Pepto Bismol and that she thought I should maybe start looking for an older, more stable girlfriend."

JANINE'S STORY

When Janine thinks about why she hasn't found a long-term relationship, she keeps coming back to the image of her mother.

"After living with my mother, how can I ever trust anybody? I feel like I was raised in a den of wolves, and I'm honestly shocked sometimes that I'm even able to have friends, let alone a solid, romantic relationship."

Janine, a researcher in her early thirties, wasn't born in the

United States. She says that several years ago she decided that she could no longer have a relationship with her mother, who lives in Canada, and she hasn't spoken to her since. Janine says that she is quick to recognize narcissism, and she makes a point of avoiding people who are self-absorbed. She had enough experience living with her mother. Describing what it was like growing up, Janine says:

"With my mother it was always me, me, and don't forget about me. My mother thinks of herself as a wonderful person, and she has this long list of wonderful things that she has done for everyone. She reminds you of all her sacrifices and kindness whenever possible. She was impossible to live with because she also had this long list of her rules and her requirements for living. They encompassed everything—the proper placement of objects, how to close doors, what to wear, what to say. If anything wasn't done exactly the way she liked it, she would immediately start in on a harangue. 'How could you do this to *me?*' was a constant refrain. She often talked about what a great parent she was. In the meantime, everyone was terrified of her, including my father. Nobody dared to confront or disagree with my mother, who was sure that she was never wrong. She has no friends, and she makes sure that my father doesn't have any friends, either. However, she comes from a large family, and as the eldest sister, my mother delights in bossing family members around."

Janine acknowledges that many of her mother's issues came from deep-seated insecurities, but that didn't make being her daughter any easier.

"Yes, my mother acted as though she was superior to everyone. But I'm positive that she really felt inferior. She had less of an education than many of her contemporaries, and she was certainly less educated than my father. To cover her insecurity, she always managed to find other people's fatal flaws, which she would point out whenever they were no longer around.

"My mother was particularly bad with me. When I became a teenager, she got really vicious. She accused me of misbehaving constantly, and she would refuse to do things for me. She would cook dinner for everyone else, for example, but not for me. If she didn't get her way, she would get furious. She would fly into rages and accuse me of having sex with everyone. *Everyone.* And it wasn't true. 'I brought you into this world,' she would scream. 'I deserve to be treated with respect.'"

Janine, who wears no makeup, is an exceptionally beautiful woman with a flawless complexion and shiny black hair. She is so extraordinary looking that it seemed natural to ask her whether she felt that her mother might have perceived her as a threat because of the way she looks.

"I think that's possible," she agrees. "My mother is very vain, and she spends a lot of time looking in mirrors and fixing herself up. When I was a kid, I was a tomboy, and I didn't think that much about how I looked. But when I was sixteen, my father sat me down and said that the reason my mother and I had a troubled relationship was that my mother was jealous of the way I looked. Well, there wasn't much I could do about that, was there?

"My entire life, my mother has been incredibly mean to me. As soon as she would look at me, I could see her getting furious. Even when I was a baby, she would do things like slap me across the face or pinch my face hard. There were a lot of flying objects in my house. She never said anything positive about me, but she had a lot of bad things to say about me and to me."

Janine says that she admits that her mother may have terrified her of any close relationships, and she hopes that this will change over time. She is currently dating someone she likes, but nonetheless Janine is very wary. She says, "When you let people close, they can really hurt you."

KYLE'S STORY

Kyle says that he went into therapy about a year ago because he became depressed when his long-term girlfriend broke up with him and almost immediately remarried her ex-husband.

Kyle says that his problem is that he seems to gravitate toward women who have a tough time with fidelity. He says:

"I like women who are exciting, I admit it. It's not so much that they have to be traditionally beautiful, because I've certainly been attracted to women who weren't. But they have to have charisma and confidence and act as if they are sure of themselves with men. Of course my last girlfriend and I broke up because she was too sure of herself with guys—way too sure.

"My therapist has pointed out to me that my last girlfriend was a textbook case narcissist. Everything had to be her way, and the minute it wasn't she threw a tantrum. She was also insanely jealous, and I don't just mean about other women. She was jealous of everybody in my family and everybody I worked with. She was even jealous of my dog and kept telling me that I should give Sadie away because she was coming between us.

"My therapist and I have started talking about my family, particularly my father, who is a pretty strong character. It's very hard for me to come to terms with the idea that my father is destructive, although objectively I can see how what he does could be described that way. It's just that my father has always told me and my brother how much he loves us, and I believe he does.

"My parents were divorced when I was ten, and we were all pretty shaken up. Among the most obviously self-centered things my father did was withhold support money from my mother. He talked about this with me at the time, explaining that it was my mother who wanted the divorce, which he thought was unfair. The main reasons why my mother wanted a divorce was that my dad had a girlfriend. My father said it was nothing serious and that my mother wasn't interested in sex. From my father's point of view, my mother was the one who broke up the marriage. I've kind of always accepted my father's point of view. Even now, although I understand how my brother and I suffered from what he did, I tend to forgive him and, in some ways, blame my mother. As soon as he walked through the door, my mother would start crying. I think it was hard for anybody to handle, so he just ran away.

"My father is the kind of guy who has an opinion about everything, and if you want to get along with him, you sort of have to go along with his opinions. That's just the way he is. If you accept that about him, you're going to get along fine. If you don't, you have a real problem. I don't agree with my father about everything. We have different opinions about politics, for example, but I'm certainly not going to open up that can of worms by telling him how I feel. My brother and father always argue because my brother won't go along with him; right now my father refuses to speak to my brother—which my brother says is okay with him.

"My father can be a lot of fun and exciting to be around. He's a salesman, and I used to love going out with him when I was a kid. It's true that he loves an audience, but he's full of funny stories and loves to do things. When I was a kid, he used to drink too much; sometimes he even took me with him to the bar. I loved hanging out with him and watching him talk to people. He told me once that he could sell anything, and I believe him. He really knows how to handle people. My mother says that he is always selling, and you can't believe a word he says. It's true that there were a lot of times when he disappointed me by telling me that he would do something that didn't happen, but I still like the guy. He's my father. He taught me how to ride horses and throw a football.

"My brother, who is also in therapy, thinks that I should look for similar patterns between my father and the women I end up liking. When I told my therapist this, she said she didn't think that was a bad idea. But I don't see it. I see the ways that he is hard to get along with, and I've tried very much not to be like him. The only similarity I see is that he was the 'exciting' parent who took us on 'exciting' outings and promised us the world. For the most part the women I've been involved with haven't lived up to what they told me about themselves at the beginning of the relationship. Is that the same thing? I don't know."

MARGARET'S STORY

At thirty-two, Margaret says that she hasn't married, although she's had plenty of opportunities, because she still hasn't found anybody who comes close to what she wants to find in a man. She says that she believes at least part of her attitude comes from her upbringing. She says:

"My parents seem happy enough together, even though my mother is often critical of my father who, by the way, pretty much humors my mother with anything she wants.

My mother is an artist who always worries too much about appearances. To say that my mom stands out in a crowd is a total understatement. She was dressing like Madonna while the Material Girl was still studying her catechism. She dresses to be viewed, and she managed to convince all her children that the world was always watching us. I remember walking into restaurants with my family, and as soon as we sat down, my mother would critique what people must have thought of us. Sometimes the critiques were positive; she would say things to my sister like, 'I could see that woman at the table near the door staring at you. I bet she wanted to know where we get your T-shirts.' Often they were negative and directed at my brother: 'When you walk funny like that, everyone thinks you're a loser.' I admit it is nuts, and she managed to create three completely self-conscious children."

Margaret was quick to tell us that her feelings about her mother were very conflicted.

"In some ways my mother is a distorted human being with strange values. She can also be very selfish. But my mother is also incredibly kind and loving and involved in our lives. She's also funny and has a wicked tongue. Years ago I made two lists. One was of all the ways that I wanted to avoid being like my mother; the other was a list of all the ways that I wanted to be like her. She's adventurous and brave, and," Margaret laughs, "she really does have a great sense of color. But in other ways she's silly and self-involved, and she can be mean. She sometimes tells mean stories about people and mimics them, like how stupid the woman at the dry cleaner was because she gave her the wrong change, or how terrible some 'chubby guy from Kansas looks with his bad toupee.'

"My mother always had something to say about everything. In my case, she commented on everything from my friends, to what I wore, to what I ate, and how I ate it.

Probably the worst thing that did to me was make me very unsure of my judgment and my decisions. Nothing is ever good enough, because I don't feel good enough. Just once I would like to walk into a room with my mother in it and not have her find something wrong with me. With my mother, though, it's always mixed. I'll walk into a room full of people, and my mother will look at me and make an announcement like, 'Look at my beautiful daughter! With that face, why can't she wear something a little less dowdy?' Then she'll pull me aside and in a loud whisper say something like, 'Don't eat any of the dessert. You're putting on weight.' Everyone hears her, of course.

"I know that whenever I meet a new guy, I can hear exactly what my mother will say about him when she meets him. It's very disruptive. One of these days I may have to learn to turn off her voice in my head. But, hey I'm still young. I'll start worrying when I turn thirty-five."

WHEN OUR PARENTS FAIL TO VALUE US FOR WHO WE ARE

Now that we are adults, it doesn't do us much good to spend excessive amounts of time thinking about the ways that our parents and caretakers might have failed us. What we do need to realize, though, is that all of us need to be accepted and loved for who we are. We need to be recognized, valued, and prioritized. As you read the stories in this chapter, it's easy to see the ways in which these men and women failed to get the nurturance and care that they deserved.

In narcissistic family structures, the needs of the child are never considered to be as important as the needs of the parent. The child may grow up honing all the skills necessary to please another person's demands; this child may well grow up and continue to be defined by what others expect and demand. For those of us who grew up in such environments, there are far-reaching implications. We may grow up, move away, and eventually come to understand and forgive our caretakers and our families, *and this is a good thing*. Nonetheless, we are still left with those internalized voices and attitudes that influence and shape how we will choose our romantic partners and how we will behave in those relationships.

Nine

WHY IS IT SO EASY FOR ME TO LOVE A NARCISSIST?

CHILDREN WHO GROW UP IN A NARCISSISTIC ENVIRONMENT inevitably end up confused about love and what it means. It's almost impossible to be the child of a narcissist and not lay claim to a fundamentally unhappy childhood. Children of narcissists know that there are old dramas playing out in their heads that desperately need to be resolved.

People who love destructive partners often explain their choices with a single word, "chemistry." This is actually a pretty good answer. Organic chemistry is all about physical fit. Two molecules will either recognize each other and fit together like puzzle pieces, or they will ignore each other. It's like a space vehicle and a docking system. Without the right configuration, the vehicle can't dock. Our history has hardwired us to recognize certain kinds of approaching vehicles. When would-be narcissistic partners approach, they look familiar. They are the missing puzzle pieces we recognize all too well; they look and act like family. We react with, "Wow! It's chemistry!!! I'm in love!!!!"

As children of narcissists, we have never really known the right kind of attention and support; we have never experienced balanced love or acceptance. We don't know what it feels like. For the most part, our ideas about love and acceptance come from our idealized fantasies. Some of the psychology books that we've read on this subject say that the children of narcissists grow up believing that they are unworthy of love. We tend to disagree with that point of view. We feel that the children of narcissists feel as deserving of love as the next guy, but they tend to look for love of the dramatic, over-the-top variety because this plays into fantasies that are spun in a love-deprived environment.

Men and women who were rarely prioritized and failed to receive a healthy dose of unconditional love as children have an extremely difficult time making wise romantic choices. Sometimes they find it easier to move toward situations that repeat the original drama and environments that leave them feeling as though they are scratching and clawing for crumbs of love. They are accustomed to feeling as though they will have to earn every bit of love they get. If it comes too easily, they don't understand it and often don't value it.

LOOKING FOR ACCEPTANCE AND NOT GETTING IT

Tammy, a thirty-seven-year-old bank manager, says that she has rarely been attracted to men who don't have an "edge." When she thinks about her relationship history, she recognizes that she has chosen very difficult partners. This has caused her much grief and heartbreak. Currently, she is trying to get over a very painful relationship with a man named Philip. From the moment that Tammy met Philip, she felt as though she already knew him for most of her life; she was convinced that they were meant to be together. She thought Philip was her soul mate; when she was with him, her world felt complete. But now, as far as she is concerned, the off-and-on romantic relationship they have shared for the last seven years is finally over. Of course their relationship will never fully be over, because Philip is also the father of Tammy's three-year-old son, Jared.

Right now, Tammy and Jared live in New York City and Philip lives in Florida.

When Jared was born, Tammy and Philip were sharing an apartment and Tammy expected that they would soon be married. However, before their son was six months old, Philip suddenly announced that he felt that his career opportunities were limited in New York City; he wanted to move back to Florida where he would also be closer to his two teenage daughters from a previous marriage. Philip had never really bonded with their son, and he didn't seem to think it was at all strange that he would leave the two of them alone in New York. He also didn't suggest that Tammy move with him. His excuse was that, at the age of thirty-nine, he wanted to go back to school; he felt that a wife and baby would "limit" his possibilities.

Philip had been threatening to leave for months, so by the time he got into his rental car and drove off, Tammy was heartbroken. Without Philip she felt as though she was missing an essential part of her very being. She also felt totally betrayed. She didn't understand how and why he could have done this to her.

Several months after Philip's departure, Tammy ran into an old boyfriend, and they started to date. Tammy's heart was never really into this, because she felt so totally committed to Philip that she really couldn't consider anyone else. This pairing also never really had time to get off the ground, because Philip heard about it from a mutual friend, and that was all he needed to reappear in Tammy's life.

For the last two years, Tammy and Philip have spent hours on the phone, negotiating and renegotiating their relationship. Tammy says that, during this time, no matter what had happened between them in the past, she was convinced that they had a unique and karmic connection. The things that Philip said to her only reinforced that belief. Whenever they spoke, Philip was very emotional and passionate; he managed to weave a cocoon around the two of them, saying that if they were together, nothing else mattered. The implication was always that their relationship was "special." Tammy has consistently been amazed at Philip's ability to impact her emotions. When she is near him, she feels electrified. When Philip is loving, Tammy feels ecstatic; when Philip is critical, Tammy feels decimated.

Philip said that he wanted nothing more than to find a way for the two of them to be together again. Philip spoke about moving back to New York eventually. However, for the moment, he thought he would do better in Florida and pleaded with Tammy to come to Florida and be with him. Tammy, who has a job, a rent-stabilized apartment, and several supportive siblings in New York City, was very nervous about picking up and moving to Florida. Tammy's hesitation has been fueled in part because Philip left her once before and he doesn't have a steady work history. When Philip is employed, he makes a very generous salary. However, more than once he has announced that his superiors were fools and has either quit or precipitated an argument that got him fired.

Philip's pattern was that he called Tammy every day about 6 P.M., often in tears about how much he missed her and their son. They were also flying back and forth between New York and Florida for vacations and long weekends. It was exhausting, and Tammy finally agreed to move. She would give notice at her job and start trying to find one in Florida. In the meantime, Philip would find a place for the two of them to live.

A few weeks ago, on Valentine's Day, Philip called Tammy at his regular time, and they talked about their plans. As he was hanging up, Philip said, "I just want you to know that I love you, hon." When they were finished talking, Tammy thought to herself, *I think I finally trust him again.*

At 8 P.M. that night, while she was carrying her son to bed, Tammy slipped and badly hurt her foot. It turned out to be a sprain, but at the time she was sure it was broken. She got one of her sisters to stay with her son while another went with her to the emergency room. The accident made her even more aware of how much she missed Philip; she called him from her cell phone in the taxi on the way to the hospital to tell him what happened and also to tell him how happy she was that she had made the decision to move. But he wasn't there. She called him again when she got home from the hospital after eleven o'clock. The phone woke Philip's eighteen-year-old daughter, who was staying in Philip's apartment.

"Is your dad there?" Tammy asked.

"No."

"Can you have him call me when he gets home. Anytime. I really want to talk to him."

"I don't know if he's coming home tonight."

"Why, where is he?"

"He's at his girlfriend's house."

Tammy felt as though she had been run over and began to visibly shake uncontrollably. She tried to sound calm as she asked the next question. "What girlfriend?"

"Gloria," his daughter answered. "The same one. He's been with her for more than a year."

Tammy has no idea why Philip's daughter told her the truth, but Tammy is grateful that she did.

Tammy immediately tumbled into depression. Not only did she feel crushed, she felt like a complete fool. Why had she believed him? Why was she so easily duped by a man who had hurt her before?

When Tammy finally confronted Philip a day later, at first he denied that Gloria existed. Then later he admitted it, but he blamed Tammy for "creating trouble" by spying. The problem, as far as he was concerned, was that she had phoned and some-how "pried" the information from his daughter. He quickly twisted the situation so that it was somehow Tammy's fault.

Tammy didn't have enough money to go into therapy, but she felt that she needed some guidance or help, so she called an old friend who had become a social worker. Tammy's friend met her for coffee and heard Tammy's story. After she was finished listening to everything Tammy said, the friend said, "Listen, this is a no-brainer. The guy is a textbook narcissist."

The next day Tammy's friend copied the applicable pages from several psychology textbooks and faxed them to Tammy's office. Tammy said that she was stunned. It was as though the people who wrote the books knew Philip. That's when Tammy began to search for as much information as she could find about narcissism in general.

Tammy will probably always have to maintain some connection with Philip because they have a child in common. Philip was never generous with child support, but now that the relationship has ended, he is sending the barest minimum. Nonetheless, even now, sometimes when they speak on the phone, she finds herself being pulled into his orbit and responding to his world view. Even as he makes promises and spins stories that she now recognizes as being self-referential and narcissistic, Tammy frequently finds herself responding, and she has to pull back and remind herself how destructive Philip has been in her life.

With all of the reading she has done in the last few months, Tammy feels as though she has taken a crash course in narcissism. She has learned enough to know that something in the dynamic of her own family set the groundwork for the way she responded to Philip. She doesn't want to have another relationship like this one and realizes that she had better learn more about how she evolved into someone whose expectations prepared her for a narcissistic partner.

She sees similarities between the way she responds to Philip and the way she responded to her parents while she was growing up. "My mother was often unhappy and moody when I was a child," she explains, "and I felt somehow responsible for making her feel better. If I thought I did anything wrong, I was devastated at the idea of contributing to her unhappiness. I assumed much too much responsibility. No matter what I did or didn't do, it never made my mother happy, and I hated the way that made me feel. I take another person's dissatisfaction very personally. Philip was never happy. As far as he was concerned, one minute I was wonderful, the next I was a horrible, demanding person. Nothing I ever did was good enough. Instead of walking away, I kept trying to prove myself. I kept trying to get his love and acceptance, and when it didn't happen, I tried even harder, just like when I was a kid."

TAKING A LOOK AT YOUR OWN FAMILY DYNAMICS

Children who are raised in narcissistic families have parents or caretakers who are not always able to respond appropriately to a child's needs or wants. These caretakers are typically so self-involved that they have a difficult time accepting a parental role. In a narcissistic family structure, roles often become confused. This happens most often when the emotional needs of the parent are so great that they dwarf those of the growing child. How can a parent who is riddled with a toxic combination of entitlement and insecurity be mature enough to care first and foremost about the welfare of the child?

Narcissist parents leave us primed for narcissistic partners. Because narcissistic parents fail to give enough of the right kind of attention and love, their children tend to be needy, even if they aren't exactly sure of what it is that they need. Narcissistic parents demand and grab a lot of attention for themselves. Sometimes they even use their children as a way of grabbing attention. Those of us who are their children are accustomed to a dynamic in which we are incredibly accustomed to trying to please someone else. We carry that attitude and dynamic with us.

In a narcissistic family structure, the emotional needs of at least one of the parents are so great that the only way children can survive the situation is by swallowing or submerging much of their own sense of self. Sometimes this dynamic is easy to spot because one or more of the children has obviously been assigned the role of parental emotional caretaker. Often, however, it is quite subtle.

Here are some questions to ask yourself about the people who took care of you when you were a child.

• **Did either of your parents have an exaggerated or grandiose sense of self-importance that wasn't supported by reality?**

Think about how your parents interacted with the world. Did either of them show signs of an exaggerated self-importance? Did your parents condition you to believe this distorted version of reality? This behavior is sometimes very obvious: Jed's father, for example, tends to ignore his family, spending most of his spare time reclining in bed where he phones or e-mails radio call-in shows, hoping to get a chance to spout his political opinions. At dinner, the entire family is subjected to long and boring recitations of how and why Dad is smarter than any of the paid pundits. Nobody ever tells Dad that he is boring or that few people in the larger world care very much about his opinions. His children have been trained to go along with Dad's monologues. It's just the way Dad is.

A self-important view of oneself can also be very subtle. Jennifer's mother, a real-estate attorney, never has time to attend any of Jennifer's school functions. Jennifer has also been taught not to call her mother at work. Jennifer's mother considers her time too valuable. The unspoken message is that Jennifer's mother is so important that her schedule and priorities always come first. Jennifer has always made excuses for her mother. She tells herself, *My mother is busy, and she does have an important job.* By the time Jennifer is an adult, she is so trained to thinking first about somebody else's needs that it doesn't even occur to her that there is another way. She is also totally accustomed to making excuses for those she loves.

Children of narcissistic parents often grow up overly accustomed to catering to another person's moods and priorities. This can make them susceptible to romantic partners with grandiose ideas about their own importance.

• **Were your parents preoccupied with fantasies of extraordinary success, wealth, power, beauty, and love?**

Think about your childhood. Were the people taking care of you grounded in reality or did they live in fantasy worlds of their own creation? Did they draw you into their fantasy world with them?

Some children from narcissistic families, for example, describe parents who were always spinning dreams about tomorrow. Sometimes those parents only seemed to come alive on special occasions, when they were able to act out some of their fantasies. Libby, for example, remembers a mother who was always depressed until she was invited to a party. She says, "My mother would be unable to get out of bed for weeks. Then there would be some social function, and she was up and running, trying on clothes, doing makeup. She would sweep out the door, flirting with my father, who would later joke that she flirted just as much with every other man in the room."

Others remember parents who had unrealistic, grandiose, and fantasy-driven attitudes toward money. Annie says, "My father was a contractor who lived for the big jobs and the big checks. In between we would eat peanut butter, but whenever he landed a new contract for a couple of weeks we would be going to restaurants every night. My father would love that. He loved to act as though he had money to burn. Sometimes my father would put up luxurious spec houses. We got to live in the new houses, while he worked on still another newer one until he found a buyer for the old one. He *really* loved that. He loved to pretend that we could afford all that. My mother went along with it. She always hated it when we had to move, though."

In some families, a fantasy view of the world is combined with one or more addictions; it may also be combined with an unrealistic approach to money and finances. Sometimes issues with fantasy come out in the dreams parents spin for their children. Such parents may encourage their offspring to avoid the real world by telling them that they are destined for "stardom." Such parents don't want "normal" lives for themselves, and they don't want them for their children.

Children who grow up with parents who have a shaky view of reality are probably more easily attracted to romantic partners who paint rosy pictures and promise the world. This attraction to fantasy may be the single most important reason why some of us are drawn to narcissistic partners.

• **Did your parents believe that they were special and unique and could only be understood by other special people?**

Many men and women remember narcissistic parents who seemed disdainful of many of the regular folk who lived and worked in their neighborhood. Nancy remembers that her mother always insisted that they buy Nancy's clothes in a big city about an hour away from where they lived. Nancy said that all the other girls in her class were wearing jeans and T-shirts while she was wearing expensive suits from Saks. Nancy said that her mother discouraged her from dating local boys and always told her that she should hold out for a real man with sophistication and money. Nancy attended an exclusive, all-girl's camp in the summer; in the winter her mother kept her busy with music and dance lessons. The one time a local boy asked Nancy out, her mother told her she couldn't go. Nancy says that the end result was that she internalized her mother's fantasies about being "better" than most people. As an adult, Nancy has had her heart broken a couple of times by men who fed into her fantasies.

Jackson said that although his family didn't have much money, his mother insisted on enrolling him in a fancy private school. The school she selected was almost an hour away, and the entire experience made Jackson miserable. Jackson's mother was unrealistic in many ways: she showed him *once* how to take the necessary buses and subways to his school. From that point on, he was on his own. This started when he was eight years old. Jackson's daily trip was exhausting as well as scary. His schedule meant that he didn't get to play with the neighboring kids, so he didn't really get to make any friends. When he complained to his mother, she reminded him of how she wanted the best for him.

Parents who believe that they and their children are "special" run the risk of making their children feel lonely and alienated from their own peer group. Kids like this often grow up believing in the soul mate fantasy; because they are special, they are fated for special lives in which they will meet and fall in love with other special people.

• **Did either of your parents always set things up so that they got most of the attention and their priorities came first?**

Parents of the look-at-me/pay-attention-to-me variety continue to take over our lives long after we've grown up and moved away from home. In some households the parent who always wants center stage is easy to recognize. The father who pontificates, the mother who always has to have the last word, the parent who competes with his/her children at every opportunity—these are all obvious examples. But in some families, a parent's need for admiration is not so immediately discernible. Megan says that her mother was the perfect martyr. "My mother got everybody's attention because she always sighed and looked miserable. She loved to do things that made her stand out for all she accomplished—the most homemade cookies, the biggest Christmas dinners. She did it all, and she made us pay a terrible price. She wanted us all to be totally grateful all the time. She wanted us to thank her a thousand times a day. It's hard for me to explain how my mother drove her children crazy. Nobody could see it. But we all could feel it. We were supposed to worship at the feet of her martyrdom."

Theo says that the one thing he remembers most about his mother's need for attention was that she never let him (or anyone else) speak. "My whole life, I rarely tell my mother anything because she never gives me a chance," he says. "She's always telling her stories. Even today when I call my mother, she immediately starts in with a story from her life. She barely asks how I am. I really hate calling her for that reason."

Parents who need a great deal of attention frequently don't know how to attend to their offspring. Children who grow up in this kind of environment may never learn how to shine on their own. They can grow up feeling unloved and as though nobody pays attention to them.

• **Did your caretakers have an over-the-top sense of entitlement? How did this affect you?**

Let's look at some of the ways a sense of entitlement impacts on parenting. For example, narcissistic parents often think that they are "entitled" to perfect children. When her children misbehave or get into any kind of trouble, the narcissistic parent is the first to feel or actually say, "How could you do this to *me?*" Parental entitlement sometimes shows itself in the expectations a mother or father has for their children. Mitch says, "My parents thought they were entitled to a son who would get great grades, go to medical school, get married to someone of the same faith, and produce grandchildren while they were still young enough to enjoy them. Of course they never asked me what I wanted to do."

Kandi says that her mother "felt she was entitled to a beautiful daughter. That was the most important thing in her life, and because of it, she made my life hell. She wanted me to look like Julia Roberts. From the moment I woke up in the morning until I went to bed at night, she talked to me about how to make me more beautiful. She had me on a strict diet when I was eight, and I wasn't even overweight!"

Parents with entitlement issues may also feel little need to adhere to normal societal expectations of parental behavior. They may want to break the "rules" and/or ignore them. A parent who thinks he is entitled to sleep late, for example, may neglect getting the children breakfast and sending them off to school. A parent who thinks he is entitled to big cars and expensive clothing may resent spending money on a child's education.

A sense of entitlement goes hand in hand with a poor understanding of boundaries. A mother with entitlement issues might think nothing of invading her children's privacy. Isn't she entitled to read her daughter's diary? A father with disturbed boundaries might think it's normal to accompany his son on his first date. After all, he's the father. Isn't he entitled? A parent with boundary issues might think nothing of raiding a child's savings or trust account. The logic being, isn't a parent entitled? The most extreme example of bad boundaries is with those parents who in some way treat their children as sexual objects.

It's often difficult to argue with parents who have an inappropriate sense of entitlement, because little will shake their faulty logic. One of the biggest problems with this, however, is that one can sometimes later find oneself with a romantic partner whose poor boundaries and sense of entitlement are even more pronounced.

• Did your parents have a tendency to exploit others without guilt or remorse? Did they exploit you in any way?

Self-centered parents often exploit their children. Did your parents, for example, take advantage of your good nature or your desire to please? Did either of them expect you to "understand" and act like the adult, no matter how difficult it was to do so? Sometimes this kind of parental behavior is inadvertent and something over which the parents have little control. Parental illness, whether it's physical or emotional, can create a family situation that puts tremendous burdens on a child. Sarah, for example, remembers being told when she was four years old that she must never do *anything* to upset her mother, who was prone to depressions. When Sarah was in third grade, she brought home a report card that had one "satisfactory" among the "excellents." Soon after that, Sarah's mother had a series of what her family referred to as "episodes" and had to be hospitalized. Sarah blamed herself.

In some families the good-natured child appears to be "exploited" in order to serve the needs of the more demanding child. Years ago, many women felt that they were exploited because they were girls, and were thus expected to help with housework, do the dishes, learn how to iron, etc.

People who are taken advantage of children run the risk of repeating these patterns in their adult relationships.

- **Were either of your parents lacking in empathy?**

Empathy is an important quality. People who experience empathy are able to step into the other person's world and feel both their joys and their sorrows. Toxic narcissists rarely feel any kind of meaningful empathy. Growing up with parents who can't empathize is acutely painful. Roxanne, for example, grew up with a single working mom who devoted most of her nighttime hours to trying to find a new husband. Between her work and her social life, Roxanne's mom had little time for her daughter. Most of the time Roxanne came home to an empty house, made her own dinner, and went to bed with the television for company. Roxanne said that she felt totally alone. The one time Roxanne complained, her mother cried and told Roxanne that she, the child, was being selfish for not realizing that her mother needed a life of her own.

To compound this, Roxanne said she was also embarrassed to tell anybody that her mother was never home. She didn't want people to feel sorry for her, and she also didn't want to get her mother into trouble. Roxanne says that the most distressing part of this experience was recognizing that her mother was clueless as to how Roxanne must have felt. Roxanne says that she vowed that she would never be insensitive to her own children and tried to give her mother the kind of empathy that she herself wanted.

Narcissistic parents, by the way, can often be overly sensitive about their *own* problems and can have ridiculously high expectations of others; they may demand that others be totally caring, empathic, and supportive. If they fail to get this level of attention from others, they may view it as a personal attack.

Children of narcissistic parents often voice disbelief when remembering ways that their parents failed to be empathetic to their childhood experiences. Several said that what they wanted more than anything else from life was a partner who showed them the kind of love and sensitivity that they didn't get as children. However, these people often then went on to form adult attachments to romantic partners who were also markedly nonempathic.

• **Were your parents noticeably envious or jealous of what others had? Did they assume that members of the family were the object of others' envy?**

Giselle says that other people's money was one of the primary things her family discussed. "Anybody could see that my mother particularly was deeply envious of other families who had more money and stuff than we did. She talked about it all the time. However, I was also told that everyone envied our family because we were more intellectual than anyone else. It was really crazy."

Many narcissistic parents convert their envy into contempt. When someone they envy has something they want but can't get, they immediately put down the other person delivering zingers like, "It's too bad your Aunt Dorothy doesn't have any taste in clothes. She always looks like a hooker, no matter how much money she spends."

Narcissists may be so envious that it is almost impossible for them to be happy for anyone—including their own children. How about your parents? If something good happened to you, were your parents happy about it? Or did you feel that they were just a bit envious? Did either of your parents openly compete with you?

Adrianna says: "You know how most parents want their children to have a better life? Well, I sometimes think my mother wants me to have a worse life. She doesn't want me to have anything that she doesn't have. When I was little and somebody would give me a present, she would sometimes bring it back to the store and get something she wanted for herself. She was unbelievable. I have learned the hard way not to tell her when something nice happens to me, because she will then create some kind of crisis to bring the attention back to her."

Leo says that when he would bring home good grades, his father would say things like, "You think you're so smart. Let me tell you about the time I got 100 on a physics test. Now that was smart."

Children who have grown up with envious or competitive parents may end up with a distorted sense of self as well as distorted values.

• **Did your parents have an arrogant attitude? How did this impact your life?**

Often when we query someone about whether he or she had an arrogant father or mother, the answer is no. When we ask the same person slightly altered or different questions, such as, did either your mother or father act superior to others? Were they extremely judgmental of others? Were they sometimes condescending or downright contemptuous? Then, the answer almost always changes to, "Oh yes, of course."

Arrogance comes out in many ways. It's important to think about because it reflects a faulty internal attitude toward the world. Narcissists want to be supported in their opinions and demands. In order to maintain their inflated sense of self-regard, they may need to deflate or devalue others. The logic being, "If you are inferior, then I, of course, am superior." Many narcissists do this, even with their own children. The narcissistic parent, for example, may not tell his child that he, the parent, is superior. He may, however, indicate that the child is inferior.

Parents with narcissistic issues often "put down," or devalue, their children's friends, interests, grades, and accomplishments.

This helps them maintain their own arrogant attitude. Some children of narcissistic parents have experienced this level of "put down" so many times and in so many ways that they may have internalized parental attitudes. This makes them easy prey for romantic partners who are themselves arrogant, contemptuous, and condescending.

• **Was there any situation in your family that created an unusual family dynamic? Did anyone in your family have a problem which, almost by definition, meant that everything in the family revolved around this person's needs?**

Were any of your caretakers so physically ill that it seemed as if nothing else in the world mattered? Were either of your parents alcoholics or did they have any addictions? Was anyone in your immediate family clinically depressed or bipolar? Did anyone suffer from anxiety attacks? How about your siblings or other family members? Did any of them receive so much attention that there was little left for you?

In some families, one's person's needs are so great that there is little space for anyone else to feel nurtured. Under these conditions, children sometimes only receive positive reinforcement when they are also "good little caretakers," helping their parents take care of a disruptive sibling, for example, or tending to the needs of a depressed or ill parent.

Growing up in this kind of setting creates a narcissistic environment, in that a child is taught to "swallow" his or her needs. For some children, this creates resentment and anger; others fall too quickly into the good little caretaker role; still others always end up feeling needy and left out; others have all these reactions and everything in between. This can play havoc with the romantic choices one makes later in life.

Finding the narcissistic themes in our lives and our histories is the way we can change our choices and our behavior. Think about some of the ways in which you may be accustomed to being devalued. Think about the stuff that you carry with you into your relationships. This is not about getting mad, and it's definitely *not* about getting even. It's about educating yourself so that you can see some of the reasons why you might have ended up loving a narcissist; it's about educating yourself so that you can learn how to be more self-protective. And, most important, it's about valuing yourself and your needs and putting some balance back into your relationships.

Part 3

PROTECTING YOURSELF

Ten

THIS IS ABOUT YOU

IT'S TIME TO START THINKING ABOUT YOURSELF!

- *Who are you?*
- *What's most important to you?*
- *What are you looking for in a partner?*
- *Did the person you fell in love with have the qualities you wanted in a partner?*
- *Why do you think you fell in love with a narcissist?*
- *Why are you more (or less) inclined to put up with narcissistic behavior than others?*
- *How can you protect yourself in the future?*

*I*N THIS SECTION OF THE BOOK, WE'RE GOING TO ASK you to put your focus on yourself, as opposed to the narcissist you love. So pay attention because your romantic relationships are as much about you as they are about your partners.

We realize that not everyone who reads this book will be doing so for the same reasons, and not everyone will be approaching it from the same place. For the sake of clarity, we're going to run through some of the more common reasons why a title like *Help, I'm in Love with a Narcissist* might have struck a nerve in your psyche.

Which of the following best describes your current situation?

- Have you recently started dating someone who displays some narcissistic traits? Are you wondering whether you should bail out now before you get in over your head?

- Have you had so many relationships with narcissists that you want to find better methods of protecting yourself in the future? Are you wondering why you keep meeting these people? Are you confused about why so many relationships have gone wrong?

- Are you desperately searching for ways to improve ongoing connections with narcissistic partners? Are you tired of always being the one who accommodates and tries to please? Even so, do you feel the good outweighs the bad? Are you still trying to find ways to fix your relationships?

- Are you in deeply troubled relationships that you are thinking of ending? Has your partner betrayed you, abused you, or taken advantage of your good nature one time too many? Do you think you are finally ready to get out?

- Are you trying to recover from the traumatic breakup of a relationship with a narcissistic partner? Are you still in a state of shock, unable to stop thinking about what happened and what went wrong?

Whatever your reasons for reading this book, we'd like to start with a very large message:

YOU ARE NOT GOING TO BE ABLE TO FIX, CHANGE, CURE, OR HEAL THE NARCISSISTS IN YOUR LIFE!

People who fall in love with narcissists frequently end up investing enormous amounts of time trying to analyze and understand their partners' behavior. Take Chloe, for example. Chloe devotes large chunks of her time to trying to learn more about narcissism. She has a bookshelf filled with purchased volumes about relationships and human behavior; whenever she has the chance, she goes online searching, always searching, for more information. When she finds new material on the Internet, she prints it out; there are stacks of these printouts hidden away in a filing cabinet.

Chloe is trying to understand more about Oliver, who has been her boyfriend for the last four years. Chloe feels as though her time with Oliver has resembled a faulty roller coaster; she wants to know why. Chloe even went into therapy a year ago so she could get some professional advice on how to "handle" Oliver. To say that Chloe is obsessed with Oliver would probably be an understatement. Every night before she goes to bed, Chloe says a little prayer asking that God or the universe or whoever else might be listening will do something to make Oliver change. So far, all of her pleas have gone unanswered.

Here's our advice for Chloe and everyone like her: if you want your relationship with a narcissistic partner to change, we want you to truly understand that the first thing you have to do is to stop thinking so much about your partner. Stop trying to understand him/her. Stop trying to analyze his/her behavior. This is about *you* and *your* life! This is about your well-being, your happiness, and your emotional survival. If you hope to transform your relationships, you are going to have to focus first on yourself. You—and only you—hold the key to your future.

We want to repeat this again to make sure that you understand. We can't find enough ways to tell you that you are not going to be able to change narcissistic partners and you are not going to be able to change their narcissistic scenarios. You are not going to be able to change their patterns; you are not going to be able to change the way they approach the world; you will not be able to change their narcissistic impulses. You will not be able to heal their intrinsic pain nor will you be able to make your narcissistic partners more empathetic. And it goes without saying that you will not be able to make much of a dent in their solipsistic views of the universe.

Perhaps you think that if you have enough information and understanding, you will somehow be able to communicate it to your partner, who will wholeheartedly accept it. Perhaps you think you will be able to convey what you have learned to your partner, who will change accordingly. Forget about it! This is not a likely scenario.

Hear this: if your partners do change, it will not come about because of anything you tell them. It will only come about because they want to change. And, for whatever it is worth, the most likely men and women to change are those whose approach to life is no longer working. The least likely to change are those narcissists who appear to get a great deal of what they want doing things the same old way.

As far as narcissists are concerned, keep this in mind:

Narcissists don't want your help.

Maybe they want your help in a weak moment. Maybe when they've hit rock bottom. But a narcissist who is not at rock bottom almost always rejects anyone who is trying to change him/her. Only the most skilled professionals have a grain of a chance at helping someone like this. There are dozens of books written about narcissistic personality disorder, and not a single one has enough words to make a genuine impact on the behavior patterns of a toxic narcissist. So if that's the only reason you're combing the library and the Internet, it's time to stop. Your partner has a problem. You can't fix it. So what are you going to do now?

Narcissists rarely change

Why not? Because a) they don't believe that they need to change; b) they don't want to change; and c) they lack the tools to change. Every bone in a toxic narcissist's body is defended against the possibility of insight and awareness. They don't want to do the work. This is their survival mechanism. Translation: this is not a motivated group.

Narcissists punish the ones who get closest

It may feel like a cliché to say, "You always hurt the one you love." But it is an ironclad truism that narcissists inflict the deepest cuts on the people they trust most. The fact that your narcissistic partner trusts you makes you the ideal target. Narcissists are afraid of abandonment; they attack those they trust because they recognize that they have found a place where they don't have to worry about abandonment. Here's another sad truth: narcissists typically don't attack until they know their partners are loyal. But then the attack is swift and devastating. When you try to get closer and show greater understanding for a narcissist's problems, there is an incredibly good chance that you will be clobbered.

Something else to take into consideration: if you are completely tolerant of your partner's narcissistic behavior, it's entirely possible that he/she will hold you at least partially responsible for their behavior—the thought being, "Well, if she didn't want me to lie, why did she put up with it?"

STOP BELIEVING IN MIRACLES—AT LEAST AS FAR AS YOUR PARTNER IS CONCERNED

This is another pretty harsh message that most of you probably don't want to hear. We realize that no matter what anyone says, many of you honestly don't believe that your partners won't or can't be different. We realize that many of you honestly believe that if you love enough and work hard enough, you will be able to create miracles.

• Nina, for example, believes that if she continues to be faithful, loving, and forgiving, her cheating, lying ex-boyfriend will change his ways and come back to her. Her friends encourage her to find somebody else, but she refuses because she feels that then she would be betraying him.

• Jessie believes that if she can learn never to nag, complain, or disagree, her disagreeable and uncooperative husband will stop being demanding and unkind. Her parents and family tell her to divorce him, but all she does is try to find more ways to please him.

• Ethan believes that if he makes enough money to pay for extra household help and learns to put up with his wife's moods and need to have everything her way, she will stop her incessant complaining about whatever he does, particularly the time he spends with his children from his first marriage. Ethan is sure that if he can only get his wife to listen to reason, he can convince her that she shouldn't be threatened by his children. But she is so deaf to his words that he can never get through.

• Nicole believes that if she loses ten pounds and makes enough money selling real estate to buy a more expensive wardrobe, her husband will stop putting her down and comparing her to the single women in his office. However, when she told him about her self-improvement plan, he said, "It doesn't matter how much weight you lose or what you wear; you'll always look like a suburban matron."

• Chuck believed that if he could get his girlfriend to go to church, she would stop sleeping with her ex-husband and lying to him about it. However once he got her to church, she developed a crush on the music director. Now he believes that if he could just get her to a shrink . . .

If you were to ask these people why they are so convinced that they can make relationships with unreasonable narcissists work, they would cite love. They would say that they believe in love. We all live in a culture that encourages us to believe in the miracle of love. Don't you believe that love will heal your relationships? Doesn't everybody? Don't we all want to continue to believe this? It's incredibly difficult to let go of this belief. Many of us remember the scene in Peter Pan where the audience is asked to clap for Tinkerbell. If the audience believes and claps, then Tink's light will grow stronger and stronger. Who doesn't want to clap for Tinkerbell? Many men and women feel that if they give up the belief that their love can heal their relationships, it's a little bit like giving up on Tinkerbell. It's like giving up on love itself. It's like becoming a nonbeliever with all that entails.

We don't want to appear to be totally cynical nonbelievers. And we're not. However, since we started writing books about relationships almost twenty years ago, we have received thousands of letters, phone calls, and e-mails from people who have been stubbornly committed to trying to please incredibly difficult partners. We feel that we can say, with an amazing amount of conviction, that this scenario is not going to end up the way you hope. It simply doesn't work. Narcissists neither appreciate nor value partners who take this approach. We also know that some of you already know that what we say is true. You've already tried everything with your narcissistic partners. You've tried logic; you've tried pleading; and you've tried pleasing—all of it to no avail.

We know, however, that some of you are still willing to go one more round; men and women in this category remain certain that they will be able to move mountains. They believe that their love is special, their relationships are special, and their partners are special. We ask this group to consider for a moment whether this point of view might not reflect their own narcissistic flaws.

Here's what we think: if you refuse to concentrate on becoming more self-protective and self-caring and continue to put all your energy into healing, changing, or enlightening your partner, you have to stop and wonder at your stubbornness. You have to start taking a better look at your own narcissistic issues.

Everyone knows that relationships are about two people. If you believe that you are so different that you can build a good relationship organized around one person (your partner) with the other (you) doing most of the work, you have to start taking a better look at your narcissistic issues. We think that if you still believe that your specialness, your partner's specialness, or the specialness of the bond you share can overcome the problems in your relationship, you have to start taking a better look at your own issues. This kind of thinking raises the possibility that you are becoming a victim of your very own narcissism. If this is the case, it's no longer about your partner, your partner's problem, or your partner's obliterating selfishness. It's now about you. It's about your refusal to see the relationship for what it is and acknowledge the limits of your partner's capacity to love and care.

Ask yourself why you think you can break all the "relationship rules"? Why do you think you can "win" against narcissism when so many others have failed? You need to look at your quest to prove that you are more special than the other people your partner has been with. And you need to examine exactly what it is you will be "losing" if you can't prove yourself to be special. Sure, you can spend the rest of your life being in an unhappy relationship and blaming your partner (and a narcissistic partner will, indeed, give you plenty of material to work with), but there comes a moment when a trip to the mirror is your greatest opportunity to free yourself from your unhappiness.

Here's the good news: although we don't believe you can change your partner, we are certain that you can change yourself. You can change your responses, and you can change the way you interact. You can become more aware of why you are so vulnerable when it comes to narcissistic romantic partners. You can get enough understanding so that you will be able to step back and get a more accurate reading on the dynamic between you and your partnes. You can become more in touch with your own tendencies to allow somebody to take over your life, and more conscious about what you bring to a narcissistic relationship.

BEEN THERE, DONE THAT

When we sound totally negative about the possibility of altering your partner's behavior, we want to make it clear that we're not being judgmental of your efforts. We both know what it feels like to hope against hope that a partner's behavior will change. We know what it feels like to spend fruitless hours looking for ways to help a narcissistic partner. We've been there; we've done that.

We know firsthand that if you want your relationships to improve, first you have to do some work on yourself. And we know that the first thing you have to change is your attitude. You have to stop thinking so much about your partner's mental and emotional health and put the focus back on yourself. This is not about being selfish. It's about being practical, sensible, and smart. This is the only way you have any hope of coming out ahead.

BEGIN BY LETTING GO OF SOME OF THE RESPONSIBILITY

Trust us: if you are involved with a narcissist, and if your relationship is going wrong or going south, you have no reason to fault yourself. Sometimes a narcissist's behavior and attitude appear so inexplicable that the only thing we feel we can do is blame ourselves. We can't find a rational explanation for what is happening. Why is the person we love hurting us? Why is the person we care about being so cruel? We try to get into the other person's head and figure it out, but it makes no sense. The only thing we can figure is that we must have done something to provoke this unkind behavior, and we assume too much responsibility for the outcome of our relationships. For example:

• Gwendolyn is very worried about her relationship with Andrew, who seems to be withdrawing from her and has become very hurtful and sarcastic in the way he talks to her. Whenever Andrew says something disparaging, she listens very carefully to his words. If she's done something to make him pull away, she wants to know what it is. Even more important, she wants to do whatever she can to change any behavior that he finds bothersome. So when Andrew accused Gwendolyn of always finding fault with him, she listened very intently. The only problem is that Gwendolyn can't think of a single solitary instance where she found fault with Andrew. So she asked Andrew what he was talking about. He reminded her of something that happened on a rainy night when he was picking her up in his car in front of her house. when he drove up, she motioned him to go forward so that she could avoid stepping in a very large puddle. Gwendolyn can't believe Andrew could think that was finding fault. But she respects his sensitivity and is now being extra careful to not do anything that could in any way be interpreted as criticism or fault finding. So far Andrew is still withdrawing and being mean in dozens of small ways. Nonetheless, she thinks that if she never does anything that can in any way be construed as "wrong," Andrew will come to his senses.

• Emmett has a difficult time understanding the moods and demands of his wife, Jacqueline. She knew how much he earned when they got married. Yet she insisted on an expensive wedding and a condo they can't afford. Then she wanted a baby. Then she quit her job. Now she wants a bigger house. She says horrible things to Emmett about how a real man would make more money. Emmett can't believe that Jacqueline, who used to have a strong feminist presentation, could become so retro. She belittles him so much that he would leave her if it wasn't for his son, whom he adores. Even Jacqueline's family supports Emmett; they all say that her behavior is outrageous, but Emmett is not so sure. He knew his wife was a great beauty who expected a lot. Maybe it is his fault. Maybe if he could give her everything she wants, then she would become more like the woman he married.

• Marcella's self-centered arrogant boyfriend convinced her to move across country to be with him. Unfortunately, soon after she quit her job, packed up her belongings, and moved to be with him, he dumped her. He told her that he had changed his mind and didn't want an exclusive relationship with anybody. She just discovered that he is already involved with somebody else. Now she has a job she can't afford to quit in a strange city with no real friends and she can't stop crying. She desperately wants her ex-boyfriend to sit down and talk to her and try to explain what happened, but he won't even answer her phone calls. She wonders what she could have done that hardened him this way. She keeps trying to figure out why he rejected her. Could it be because she gained three pounds over the winter?

Narcissists are very persuasive—even when they are wrong or infuriatingly mercurial. No matter how twisted their reasoning or behavior, they want their partners to go along with it, and they have a sales pitch and a story to help sell you their point of view. They are invested in thinking that they are always right and never really at fault. Most of you know firsthand how quickly they blame the other guy. And they are very good at what they do.

If you are the romantic partner who is being emotionally abused, neglected, humiliated, or dumped, it's pretty safe to assume that the narcissist in your life is trying to justify his/her behavior by pinning primary responsibility on you—even if it's not done directly. Our friend Genna said that before her narcissistic and alcoholic husband stopped drinking, he would tell his friends how mean she was to him. She would join him at office parties and people would stare at her. After he sobered up, he acknowledged that he had been purposely distorting people's views of her.

The big questions are: Why are you so quick to assume responsibility? Why are you so quick to find excuses and reasons for a narcissistic partner's intolerable behavior?

WHY DO YOU THINK YOU HAVE TO BE
THE ONE TO FIX EVERYTHING?

Men and women who fall in love with narcissists are often the kind of people who want to be accommodating to others; they want to please. Sometimes they want to please the other person so much that they are willing to assume responsibility for everything in the relationship, including everything that goes wrong.

Julia remembers visiting a couple in New York City a few years back. The wife, Marie, a lawyer with a full-time job, was the major breadwinner for the household as well as the primary caretaker for her two children from her previous marriage. The husband, Anthony, was an unemployed writer who was having a hard time selling anything he wrote and was unwilling to do anything else to earn money.

On the Saturday afternoon that she visited, Julia was one of several guests. Everyone was sitting around eating the hors d'oeuvres that Marie had made and listening to Anthony complaining about publishers who didn't understand his work. Anthony seemed to be having a fine old time until he asked his wife to make him a drink with vodka in it.

"I'm sorry," Marie apologized. "We're all out of vodka."

"We don't have any more vodka," Anthony repeated in a confrontational tone.

Marie replied, "I must have forgotten."

"Well, vodka *is* what I drink," Anthony said pointedly. "I believe Jayne is also drinking vodka. In fact, I think I poured the last of the bottle into her glass," he said.

"Not to worry," Jayne replied. "I can drink or not drink anything. Besides," she added, "Marie worked hard all week. Let her sit still for a minute."

Anthony totally ignored Jayne's comment about Marie's work schedule when he replied, "Well, maybe you can drink anything, but I can't."

"I'll run right out," Marie said. "I'm sorry," she kept apologizing. "It's my fault. I should have remembered to buy it when I did the shopping yesterday."

While Marie was at the store, Anthony took the male guests into his den to show them something. When he did, Jayne spoke to Julia, saying. "Anthony is the most self-involved guy in the world. Marie has been my friend for years, and he treats her like she's his personal servant. All he talks about is himself, and he never does a damn thing to help her!"

A couple of years later, Julia met Marie in another setting and was told that Marie and Anthony had been divorced. "You know," Marie said, "Anthony just had so many needs, and no matter how hard I tried, he was never satisfied."

"Are you very upset about the divorce?" Julia asked.

"I just keep wondering what else I could have done or what I could have done differently," Marie answered.

This story illustrates one of the great difficulties of loving a narcissist. Simply put, it's just a lot of work. It's very easy to get into the habit of being the one who is shouldering most of the responsibility for maintaining the relationship. Remember, relationships are supposed to be about two people, both of whom are doing what they can to support each other. Narcissists aren't inclined to be very supportive; they tend not to accommodate or cooperate. They rarely, if ever, do more than their share.

When we are in love, it's very painful to be in a relationship with a partner who is not doing his/her share. Sometimes it's so painful that we feel we have to do something, anything, to change things. What we often hate most are feelings of being powerless. We realize that the only behavior we can control is our own. So we vow that we will love even harder and do even more in an attempt to save our relationships. It's a way of staying positive. It's a way of convincing ourselves that we still have some power. When you're in love, this seems to be a less painful plan than giving up. When we do this, of course, we organize all our energy around our narcissistic partner, which tends to reinforce the situation.

MODIFYING YOUR BEHAVIOR AND TAKING CARE OF YOURSELF

Men and women who fall in love with narcissists sometimes want to take care of others more than they want to take care of themselves. It goes without saying that this may not be the wisest way to behave. If you sincerely hope to develop better coping skills in your romantic relationships, you have to start by putting more energy and focus on yourself.

Here are some suggestions to get you started.

1. Examine what happens when you try to please your romantic partner.

Ask yourself these questions: Why are you so quick to try to take care of the other person's needs? Do you remember when you started behaving this way? Has your need to please always been your default position?

Your intense desire to please people and make them happy may be one of your nicest and most admirable traits. However, it can absolutely get you into trouble. Toxic narcissists seem to have an uncanny ability to sense people who have this trait and to take advantage of them.

There are lots of wonderful reasons for going out of our way to keep our partners happy. However, some of our reasons for doing so are not totally altruistic. Let's face it, we are kind to the people we love because we want to encourage them to treat us in the same way. There is certainly nothing wrong with taking this approach if you are dealing with someone who shares your attitude. Narcissists, however, don't typically respond the way you hope. More likely than not, they will simply take advantage of you. In fact your generosity of spirit may make them less giving—not more.

2. Examine your fears about what you think might happen if you stop trying to make your partner happy.

Here are some questions to ask yourself: What do you think will happen if you stop trying to please your partner? Do you ever give your partner a chance to do as much as you do to make the relationship work? If you stop working so hard at your relationship, are you afraid that it will disappear?

Some of us start out always trying to please others in an effort to fight off our fears of being abandoned or dumped. We think that if we are always available and do everything we can to make our partners happy, they will never want to leave us. We know a great many people who tried this approach and had it fail miserably. Narcissists tend to be a lot like Groucho Marx when he said, "I don't want to belong to any club that wants me as a member." Narcissists simply don't appreciate your efforts. Remember also that narcissists have a tough time with empathy; they aren't inclined to be sympathetic to your fears, either. More likely than not, they will use your fears as a way of controlling and manipulating you.

3. Examine how much time and energy you spend doing things that make you happy or that make your life easier or more satisfying for you.

Some questions to ask yourself: Do you spend as much time worrying about your needs as you do about your partner's? Have you ever taken money that you need for yourself to buy your partner a lavish and unnecessary gift? Do you regularly deprive yourself in order to "spoil" your partner? How often do you put your needs last? How often do you inconvenience yourself in order to keep your partner from suffering any inconvenience?

Rosa told us that she was standing in line at the DMV on her lunch hour in order to pick up her boyfriend's plates because he had neglected to take care of the paperwork in time. She had offered to take care of his plates for him because he seemed so annoyed that he had to do this, and she wanted to make his life easier. She also didn't want to deal with his bad mood. As she stood on line, she was thinking: *My own car needs an oil change; I need to get a hair cut; I have to buy a present for my mother for Mother's Day; I have to go to the bank; I have a ton of stuff on my desk that I could be finishing; I could be sitting in the park reading a book. I could be taking a yoga class. What am I doing here? What is my problem?*

The most healing thing you can do for yourself (and often your relationship as well) is to put at least as much energy and time into thinking about your own well-being as you do into your partner. For a week, keep track of your schedule. Note how much or how little of your free time is spent thinking about your own personal goals and how much time is used for taking care of your needs and your interests.

4. How about your friends and family? Are you surrounded by people who you are trying to please and placate?

Some questions to ask yourself: Are you conditioned to respond to narcissistic demands? Were you trained to please your parents or other people? Are your issues with narcissists limited to your partner? When you meet somebody who doesn't demand as much of you and is capable of having a more equal relationship, do you feel lost and without a clearly defined role? Do you sometimes feel as though you don't know how to relate? Do you have friends and family who regularly take advantage of you? Do you have friends and family who always demand most of the attention? Do you know people who always insist that everything be their way or else there is no friendship?

Some of us are drawn not only to narcissistic romantic partners, but also to narcissistic friends. If this is the case, you need to think long and hard about what you do to encourage these kinds of relationships. You need to start looking for people who are supportive and nurturing of you.

And, finally, we're going to repeat the following message several times throughout this book because we think it is such an important one: many people who have been in love with narcissists have found it wise to get some professional support in the form of counseling or therapy, even if it is short-term. This is something you might want to consider, because it can help you handle your situation and your relationship realistically. It will also help you protect yourself in the future.

Eleven

HOW THEY WIN US OVER

ON'T BEAT YOURSELF UP BECAUSE YOU HAVE BEEN attracted to—and fallen in love with—a narcissist; don't start indulging in too much harsh self-criticism or self recrimination. We live in a culture that elevates a wide range of narcissistic traits, and you're not alone in succumbing to narcissistic seduction. It's easy to be won over by narcissistic charm; it's certainly happened to the two of us.

Narcissists are often very popular—or at least very much the center of attention. Take a look at the world around you: look at the politicians and world leaders; look at some of those greedy corporate CEOs squandering everybody's money. Where do you think they rate on a narcissistic behavior scale?

Despite living in a world that often embraces the self-absorbed, self-involved, and self-referential, we're sure you want to reach a place where you are no longer vulnerable to narcissists and their manipulations. In order to do that, try to think a bit about why you are drawn to them initially and why you continue to be captivated by their shenanigans. We have thought about this a great deal and have asked a lot of people for their input. Here are some of the reasons that came out of our research, along with some suggestions as to how we can all use common sense to help us protect ourselves and stay grounded in reality.

REASONS FOR FALLING IN LOVE
WITH NARCISSISTS

1. Society places a value on narcissism and narcissistic values.

We would be divorced from reality if we discounted society's impact on how we behave. We've all watched the Grammys and the Oscars; we've all watched talk TV and reality shows; we've all listened to arrogant radio personalities and shock jocks; we've all read gossip columns and entertainment magazines; we've all watched movies with arrogant tough-guy heroes who regularly break women's hearts as well as society's rules; we've all watched television shows that feature female leads whose superficial values are considered cute and sexy; we've all heard politicians who are so enamored of their own opinions that they have lost touch with reality. Who can deny the narcissistic aura of so much of what we are exposed to on a regular basis?

Every single one of us knows people who act out their grandiosity; we are surrounded by people who reek of a sense of entitlement. Many of our politicians, leaders, entertainers, and celebrities are walking examples of narcissism, and yet they are more likely to be greeted with applause than condemnation. If we meet people who put incredible emphasis on external values, for example, and spend more on clothing than most of us make in a year, we don't think, "How narcissistic." Instead we admire their taste and beauty. Our society abounds with critics who make a very nice living devaluing other's accomplishments. When we read or hear these critics' views, we don't say, "How narcissistic." Instead we find them amusing and clever. Talk radio and television is filled with commentators whose major accomplishment is being able to talk so long and loud that nobody else can be heard. We don't say, "How narcissistic." Instead we assume that they know what they are talking about. How else could they sound so sure of themselves? We could go on, but you get the point. Society isn't helping us form solid and wise judgments about narcissism or narcissistic values.

Ask yourself what you notice and value about your current partner or other men or women who might be potential mates. Are you too easily influenced by how someone dresses or looks? Are you too easily swayed by someone who has a smooth presentation? When you meet someone new, are you able to look behind his credentials and the image he presents in order to get a real sense of the person and his emotional makeup? When you go out with someone for the first time, are you overly concerned with what others will think of your date?

You know better than anyone else which qualities you notice in others, and which you overlook. When asked what qualities we most want in future partners, we often list things like kindness and intelligence. But when we meet somebody for the first time, we can be so wowed by the presentation that we forget about what we really want.

2. Narcissists tell us that they are terrific, wonderful people, and we believe them.

Some of us believe whatever people tell us about themselves. For example:

• Baylee, an animal lover, says that when she met Randy he spent two hours telling her about his relationships with various animals. He told her that none of his friends could get over how much time and money he spent on stray animals; as an example, he said that his dog, Dagwood, was totally vicious when Randy found him on the streets. Randy said that nobody had ever been kind to Dagwood before and that he spent all his spare time convincing Dagwood to trust him; eventually the dog calmed down and was won over. Baylee was so impressed by what Randy said about himself that she was completely won over as well.

• Arnold says that when he met Joan, she told him in great detail about how she came from a poor family and had to work two jobs to get her MBA and how all of her professors loved her because she was so smart. Arnold said that he was charmed by all of Joan's stories that demonstrated how cute and plucky she was.

• Gerri says that when she met Ralph, he insisted on taking her to where he worked so she could see his large office and the signed testimonials on the walls, all from grateful clients. He then took her to a restaurant where he was greeted by name and they were shown to the best table with a skyline view.

The thing about narcissists is that they present themselves as though they are characters in an interesting novel. When they first meet you, they turn their lives into stories for your benefit. Yes, many of them are totally self-referential, but their stories can be so engaging and interesting that you want to hear more. If narcissists are intent on getting your attention, their approach will almost certainly succeed.

As an aside here, we'd like to remind you that there are also many "failed" narcissists in our world. These are the people whose attention-getting devices and stories don't work. These are the people whose favorite words in all circumstances are "I," "me," "my," and "mine." These are the people who act as though everyone should be thrilled to hear their monologues and opinions on everything from cat food to world peace. These narcissists are not as dangerous as the more subtle variety because they are easy to spot and avoid; few of us are attracted to them.

On the other hand, the narcissists who we do find attractive spin Sheherazade-like tales about themselves that we find both intriguing and amusing. That's why it would be a big mistake to assume that narcissists always tell their "stories" in a way that appears off-putting or too filled with ego. The most successful narcissists have presentations that are as charming as they are engaging. Narcissists are both the creators and the heroes of these stories. The most skilled know how to appear humble and humorous as well as dynamic and delightful.

Don't forget that some narcissistic stories are primarily designed to get sympathy. We know people with narcissistic issues who spend much of their time talking about how "worthless" they are; they manage to organize their relationships around their "insecurities" and problems. Sometimes they are surrounded by friends and family, all of whom dedicate themselves to convincing the narcissist that he/she is "great" and not lacking in any way.

If someone you have just met is regaling you with the traumas or successes of his/her life, and is doing it as though you are the first person who is hearing all this, stop and think. How often do you think this person must have told these stories? We're not suggesting that you be negative about everyone you meet and everything you're told; we are suggesting that you be totally self-protective and not arrive at any fixed judgments until you find out for yourself whether this person is as wonderful, sensitive, kind, and smart as you have been told.

3. Narcissists give us a role to play in their personal dramas and life stories.

• "I had known Perry less than thirty minutes before he began asking my advice on everything from how to decorate his apartment to how to improve his relationship with his children."

• "Brenda and I had been dating less than a week, and she had me painting her bedroom and picking her mother up from the hospital."

• "By the time Tyler and I were going out for two weeks, I had met most of his friends, his brother, his sister, his mother, his stepfather, his father, and his father's new girlfriend. By the time we were going for a month, he had included me in a joint session with his shrink so I could be brought up to speed on his "issues." By the time we were together two months, he and everything about him had taken over my life. That's one of the reasons why I was so destroyed when he dumped me after four months, saying that he wasn't ready for this much intensity."

Narcissists are typically very intense and their dramas are very compelling. They often invite us to become as absorbed in their lives as they are, and this can sometimes appear to be a very attractive invitation. We both know what it is to be drawn into a narcissist's world. We've both had it happen in romantic as well as nonromantic relationships. Years ago, when Steven moved to a new city where he knew few people, he was befriended by a neighbor. At first Steven was happy to meet this friendly person who invited him to have dinner and go to the movies. Within a short time, however, Steven realized that this new friend was completely narcissistic and manipulative and wanted to take over his life. Steven felt as though he was under siege. When Julia was in her twenties, she briefly had a narcissistic boss. Within a month, he had her baby sitting for his children and running his errands. He took over her life.

Narcissists are renowned for their rotten boundaries; they can walk in and take over. Why is this appealing? Well, if you're going through a period in your life where you are feeling lonely, troubled, or without a sense of direction, a narcissist can get you so involved with his/her life that you feel needed; you feel as though you have a purpose. Narcissists' sturm and drang can help us take our minds off our own problems; eventually their problems become our problems.

Narcissists take advantage of us when vacuums exist in our lives. When we are feeling busy, involved, creative, and self-confident, there is little room for narcissistic agendas, dramas, or demands. What we can extrapolate from this is that the best thing you can do to protect yourself from narcissists and their demands is to fill your life with things *you* enjoy doing.

4. At the beginning, narcissists often say and do everything we ever wanted a romantic partner to say and do.

• "He told me I was 'the one.' I think I'd been waiting to hear that my entire life."

• "She said that she thought all guys were jerks until she met me. She said that I was the smartest man she had ever met. She made me feel like I was some kind of Einstein."

- "He told me that my smile lit up the room, and he just wanted to sit around and bask in my warmth."

- "He seemed so excited about me. He said, 'I've never met anybody like you before. How could somebody like you like somebody like me?'"

- "He said, 'You're too precious to mess around with. You're the real thing.'"

- "She acted like we were going to be together for the rest of our lives. She kept telling me how much her mother would love me and how happy her sister was going to be that she had finally met someone. She said she had spent a vacation on this beach in Hawaii as a kid, and her whole life she was waiting to meet somebody she wanted to go back there with. She said I was that person."

- "It was a blind date. He came to my apartment. I gave him a glass of wine; he had been there for less than five minutes. Suddenly he gave me this incredibly intense stare, walked across the room, and started kissing me, like nobody had ever kissed me before or since. It was a 'Some enchanted evening,' moment."

- "She told me, 'I know this is going to seem crazy since we've only known each other two weeks, but I know I want to be with you for the rest of my life.'"

Let's face it, we all want to fulfill the Hollywood dream of having somebody fall madly in love with us. We're all waiting for it to happen to us, just like it used to happen in the movies from the 1950s. Narcissists, with their incredible need to idealize new romantic partners, make us believe that our dreams have come true. We are all most attracted to people who weave fantasies at times when our own self-esteem is on shaky ground. By telling us that we are wonderful and special, they make us believe that somebody appreciates our best qualities.

People who are confused about the nature of narcissism often ask us the same question about this. They say, "But I don't understand. I thought narcissists wanted us to pay attention to them. I thought they wanted us to tell them what they wanted to hear." The answer to that question is, "Yes, that is true, but first they have to get our attention."

One of the things narcissists accomplish when they idealize you is getting you to notice them.

It's easy is to be swept away by somebody who says and does all the romantic stuff we all dream about. But think about how likely you would be to display this degree of surety with a new partner. People who behave this way are sometimes less sincere than they are "smooth" and "practiced." So be realistic, practical, and wary as you approach new relationships.

5. Narcissists appeal to our own fantasies of grandeur and greatness.

Narcissists usually want to travel in the "right" circles; they want to hang out with the "right" people; they want to live in the "right" space in the "right" environment in the "right" neighborhood.

It's important to understand what we mean by "right." Not all narcissists are money-oriented or greedy or have crummy values. Some narcissists, for example, want to emulate Donald Trump; others view Albert Schweitzer as their role model; still others prefer Mother Teresa. Narcissists are defined not by their value systems, but by their sense of grandiosity and attention-getting behavior. Many narcissists are dedicated do-gooders. Narcissists are just as likely to be found working for charity organizations building homes for the impoverished as they are in large corporate offices. However, no matter where narcissists work and play, they are still going to be trying to round up as much attention as possible. The "right" place for a narcissistic performance artist in New York City, for example, might be a totally grungy loft in Brooklyn's worst neighborhood, because in some circles that has a lot of cachet.

On some level we may all have at least a few grandiose fantasies of greatness or at least hanging out with the right people. You can start protecting yourself from narcissists and their grandiose dreams by being honest with yourself about your own fantasies. If there is something you want to accomplish, set a goal and make a plan. Don't rely on your connection to another person. You don't want to be in a place where a narcissist can use your dreams of greatness to manipulate you.

6. Narcissists make us feel special by association.

The narcissistic seduction often feels like it's an invitation to greatness. The unspoken (or spoken) promise is "I'm special; you're special; together we'll be even more special." Narcissists seduce us by making us feel that we are privileged to be allowed into their lives; they tell us that we are unique, which is why we are being allowed into their lives.

Dean, a thirty-nine-year-old Web site designer, says that he knows that he has narcissistic issues and traits and that he believes it started when he was growing up. He says, "My mother always made a point of separating me and my brothers from other people. We were the special ones. We were different. Everybody else was nice enough, but we honestly grew up thinking that we were in some way superior. Then, a few years ago, I was with a friend at a party. He pointed out to me that I had a 'narcissistic habit' of shooting a 'knowing glance' to my friends as a way of communicating a feeling of superiority. It was a way of quietly saying to my friends, 'We're different. We're the smart ones. We're special.' At least that's the way it felt until my friend called me on it and labeled it narcissistic. I felt busted and deflated. Someone had seen me doing something that I had been doing for as long as I could remember. But he put a name to it. Once it was pointed out to me, I immediately knew exactly what he meant. My 'knowing glance' was a gesture that was loaded with contempt, loaded with feelings of superiority, loaded with feelings that, in my mind, set me and my friends apart from others. It was a narcissistic gesture, and I was guilty as charged."

Narcissists can make you feel as though you are so superior that you rise above the masses. When a narcissist is intent on getting someone's attention, he/she often conveys a message that says, "You and I both know something that everybody else doesn't know." Narcissists give the people they want to attract what amounts to a conspiratorial emotional narcissistic wink. It says: you belong to a special circle, and the others don't.

Building your own sense of self and self-esteem is the way to protect yourself from this narcissistic ploy. Strengthen your real connections to family, friends, and community, and you will be less likely to be attracted by the narcissistic wink.

7. Narcissists often do the things we wish we could do.

- "Melissa quit school to play the harmonica in a girl's country western band. It was probably the worst band in the history of country music, but she still talks about it like she was Faith Hill."

- "We were in the supermarket last night right before closing, and there were no eggs left on the shelves. I went to the manager and complained. The manager said, 'Sorry, but it's late.' My boyfriend didn't accept that explanation. He went to the manager and insisted that they not close until somebody went downstairs, opened up the boxes down there, and found some eggs. The supermarket ended up closing ten minutes late, but we got the eggs."

- "Gary is a wild man who isn't afraid of taking chances. I would never dream of quitting a good job just because I don't like my boss. Gary has done it three times since I met him."

Some narcissists present a picture of adventure and of not being afraid to state what they want. They can seem fearless and brave and outrageous. They can seem like the funny or glamorous characters we see on the big and small screens.

Think about Frank Sinatra singing "My Way." Narcissists appear to be people who are following their own paths; they can seem to be embodiments of every self-help message that speaks of risk and dreams. From a distance it seems attractive. Up close and personal, to live with such a person can be hellish.

Some people are also attracted to men and women who exude bravado because they think that these people will defend them. Let us assure you that this is not likely to happen. We live in a time when people admire a John Wayne kind of swagger, forgetting that John Wayne had script writers who were making up Wayne's attitude and words as they went along. Before we follow somebody like this, we need to be certain that there is some real substance and depth beneath the swagger.

We are all at least a little bit in awe of somebody who announces, "I'm going to do that," and then goes out and tries to do it. Sometimes this behavior is merely funny and little bit devil-may-care. Other times, it can end up harming others. The question to ask yourself is why you admire reckless behavior. Why do you admire people who don't worry about consequences or putting others out? Reckless behavior can take other people down. So be careful.

8. Narcissists are rarely boring (at first).

Mel and Naome have something in common. They are both recovering from abusive relationships with narcissistic partners, and they both still think their exes are completely fascinating. In fact, neither of them can stop talking about them. Why is that? Why do so many of us find narcissists interesting?

Narcissists interest their romantic partners for all the reasons we've already discussed. They draw us into their worlds; they tell us what we want to hear; they engage us in their dramas; they include us in their fantasies. Another reason narcissists are interesting has to do with an appearance of intensity and passion.

Some people also find narcissists interesting because they tend to talk about themselves. Women particularly find this a very attractive quality. Women like being with men who aren't afraid to discuss their lives, their feelings, and their dreams. Men who prefer to be quiet in social situations sometimes prefer talkative women because there is less of a demand on them.

When you go out with a narcissist for the first time, and he/she is trying to make an impression, it's unlikely that there will be big lapses or awkward pauses in the conversation. The narcissist will fill those spaces up. When their relationships are new, narcissists appear to be doing most of the work in getting things off the ground. Narcissists like to seduce new people, and when somebody is paying a lot of attention to you, it's rarely boring. When narcissists are in an idealistic mode, they can be fearless about spinning fantasies about a future that will include you. They talk about things you will do together and how much fun you will have. Later, of course, once they are in a devaluing phase or acting out a sense of entitlement, you will feel as though you are doing all of the work maintaining the relationship.

Keep in mind that being in a long-term relationship with a narcissist will eventually become boring. You will get tired of hearing the stories; you will get tired of the sense of entitlement; you will get tired of the lack of empathy; and you will get tired of the testing and attention-getting behavior. You will probably also discover over time that a narcissist's emotions are quite shallow and that all that passion and intensity is mostly facade.

9. Narcissists appeal to our own narcissistic issues.

You don't have to be a toxic textbook narcissist to have narcissistic vulnerabilities. We all have them. We all have that narcissistic "Achilles' heel." We want to feel special, better, and different. We don't want to be invisible. We don't want to be just one of indistinguishable billions who walk the planet. And that makes us vulnerable to the promises and powers of the destructive narcissist.

The narcissist's world is a very seductive one. When we are part of it, we can feel more alive and special than we could possibly feel on our own. Their grandiosity elevates us. But what goes up too high will invariably come down, and you have probably picked up this book because you feel that elevator falling right now.

All of us have narcissistic vulnerabilities. Part of healing ourselves and our relationships is recognizing how our own narcissistic hopes can contribute to getting involved in nightmarish narcissistic relationships.

Twelve

STILL TRYING TO MAKE IT WORK

OVER THE YEARS WE'VE RECEIVED MANY LETTERS from our readers (mostly from our women readers) who say that they know how stress-producing their significant others are, but they don't care. They want to do whatever they possibly can to make their relationships work. The questions these people ask are all about trying to modify their loved ones' behavior. They are looking for guidelines and help.

We'd love to be able to tell you that we have a bag full of tricks that comes complete with a guarantee for success, but we don't. Psychiatrists, psychologists, counselors, therapists, and social workers all recognize the problems of trying to alter narcissistic behavior. They also recognize how difficult it is for partners of narcissists to change the way in which they relate to their loved ones. Nonetheless, the best chance you have of becoming more comfortable in your relationship is to start by modifying your own reactions and your own behavior.

Here are some suggestions on how you might be able to bring about change.

SUGGESTION: DON'T BE CONFUSED BY YOUR PARTNER'S TWO-SIDED PERSONALITY

When you love a narcissist, you often feel as though you are in love with a Jekyll and Hyde look-and-act-alike. One moment your partner is cold, demeaning, and downright cruel; the next he/she is needy and dependent. One moment, your partner appears to want distance; the next he/she is inviting even greater intimacy. One moment he/she seems arrogant and demanding; the next he/she appears insecure and/or shy. One moment he/she seems strong and confident; the next he/she discloses amazing fears and insecurities. One moment he/she is contemptuous of just about everybody; the next he/she is astonishingly compassionate to a stranger on the street.

We need to say this one more time: narcissistic personalities tend to display two different sides, depending upon whether they are feeling "puffed up" and "inflated," or "defeated" and "deflated." Your problem in dealing with these personalities is to learn to distinguish which side of the personality is being presented to you at any moment. Your bigger problem is realizing and acknowledging that neither the "inflated" or "deflated" side is fixed in place.

What usually happens when you are in a relationship with a narcissist is that you love one side of the personality and are confused and/or a bit frightened of the other. You want to encourage one side of the personality and assume that the other side is not the "true" or real person whom you think you know best.

Paula, for example, says that when she met Danny, he seemed to be a confident, ethical man with a take-charge personality; she liked that because it made her feel as though he could take care of her. She envisioned a future with him in which she would feel secure and loved. But Danny had another side to his personality, and that side couldn't hold a job and was often in some kind of a pickle because of something he had done.

Eventually she discovered that he was chronically unfaithful, but not until after they had a child together (who Danny fails to support). Nonetheless, Paula says that when she speaks to Danny, he often assumes his loving, intimate, take-charge personality. Even today, when it has been proven to her time and time again that Danny will fail her, Paula is shocked when he doesn't honor his words or commitments.

Gus fell in love with Keisha, who is a second-grade teacher, because she seemed so serious and sincere. But as Gus gets to know her better, he is discovering that Keisha has a whole other side to her personality. That side is vain, flirtatious, and drinks so much that Gus is concerned that she is just shy of being labeled an alcoholic. Gus likes to think that this side of Keisha only comes out with certain people and that if he could steer her away from the "bad" influences in her life, Keisha would be the ideal wife and mother to any children he might someday have. She does, after all, work with small children.

Many people who are in love with narcissists have reactions to their partners that are similar to those expressed by Paula and Gus. If your partner is a narcissist:

- Stop and think about which aspect of his or her personality you fell in love with. Think about the ways that you excuse or forgive the part you don't like.
- Think about how you may blame your partner's friends or family for encouraging the behavior you dislike.
- Think about how you may have created unrealistic fantasies about your partner "abandoning" or "getting rid" of these qualities.

For those of you who are in love with narcissists, the fact remains that you are in love with people who have inflated *and* deflated sides to their personalities. We don't personally think that you and your love will be able to help your partners integrate these aspects, and we don't think it's a good use of your time to try to do so. However, we do think that you should always be aware of your responses, and we think you should come to terms with unrealistic thinking about how your partner will miraculously get rid of the part you don't like.

SUGGESTION: START ESTABLISHING BOUNDARIES

If you are going to deal with narcissists, you have to be very, very conscious of boundary issues and what they mean in your life. Every day in every way, we are all involved with negotiating our boundaries. For example, take a look at Rob, who is seated at a table in a diner with his girlfriend, Aretha. Rob seems so happy as he looks up at the cheerful waitress placing the order of hand cut French fries in front of him. Yum, they look delicious. It doesn't even occur to him that a boundary issue is about to occur. Then before the plate of French fries even hits the table, a right hand reaches out and grabs a fry. The hand is attached to Rob's girlfriend, Aretha. Her left hand is already holding the ketchup bottle, preparing to squirt. Looking at the hand, he wants to pick up his plate, clutch it to his chest, and move to another table.

At one time or another, who hasn't wanted to scream, "Get your own damned order of fries!" We feel this way because our boundaries are being crossed. The thing about boundaries is that while no man (or woman) is an island, we each have our own little universe. We feel somehow connected to our space, our friends, our work, our family, our pets, our money, our schedules, and our time. We want to protect these things; we don't want to feel invaded. If you are in love with a narcissist, be prepared to have your boundaries trampled on time and time again.

Boundary issues are one of those things that most couples work out over time. Take Jacob and Janet, for example. They have been married twenty-five years. Janet feels comfortable going through Jacob's pockets at night looking for change for parking meters. Jacob feels comfortable walking into the bathroom when Janet is soaking in the tub. They share children, a bed, a bank account, and even an e-mail address. This is where they are after twenty-five years of living together.

If Jacob and Janet were out on their second date, and Jacob was to go through Janet's pocketbook looking for an aspirin, everyone would be legitimately appalled by the inappropriateness of this act. One of the components of intimacy is that there are fewer boundaries. But it takes time and work to get there.

A boundary is inappropriate if it does any of the following:

- Forces or assumes too much intimacy or co-mingling.
- Usurps, invades, or takes over the other person's life.
- Fails to respect the other person's reasonable priorities and values.
- Creates a barrier so high and deep that there is no place for a meaningful relationship or friendship to develop.

Narcissists have trouble distinguishing between self and other. This means that almost by definition, *a narcissist is going to have inappropriate boundaries*. In fact, narcissists can seem almost oblivious to invading others' boundaries even as they protect their own. By the way, it doesn't matter whether these boundaries are physical, emotional, financial, material, psychological, or sexual. Geo, for example, started his relationship with Jane with an all-out sexual seduction that was as inappropriate as it was exciting. His immediate off-the-wall passion made Jane feel as though he was so attracted to her that he would never look at anybody else—ever. Jane was so flattered and excited that she overlooked the inappropriate aspects of his approach. It took Jane months to discover that this has been Geo's modus operandi with every woman he finds attractive, and Geo finds a lot of women attractive.

Now that they are together as a couple, Geo regularly arrives at Jane's apartment with his computer, his sports equipment, his large drooling dog, Howie, and sometimes two or three friends as well. As soon as Geo walks through Jane's door, he spreads out his belongings, throws Howie's bowl along with some crumbly biscuits on the squeaky clean floor, turns on the television, opens the refrigerator, and complains that Jane doesn't have the right brand of orange juice. Last week, when Jane borrowed some of Geo's shampoo without asking, he got annoyed.

Boundaries Define Our World

When we were infants and toddlers, our world was not our own. Someone was always wiping our faces, taking our hands, putting on sweaters, giving us food without asking whether we wanted it. As we matured, we moved away from that state. We began to discover our own separateness. We learned to say no. But this developmental process is not a perfect one. Some of us got stuck in the place where there is no separateness between the caretaker and the child. Others got stuck in the defiant "no" stage. Still others spend their lives slipping back and forth between the two and have no healthy middle ground. This group is very confusing: one moment they are treating their friends and mates as though they are parents with whom they want to feel a complete and infant- like merger, then the next they do an aboutface and behave as though they want a totally separate experience.

How we structure boundaries in our own lives depends at least in part upon the culture in which we grew up. In some families, everyone maintains a separate, independent life. In other families and cultures, independence is not celebrated; everyone is in everyone else's business. If you grew up sharing space with siblings, you are probably going to have a different idea about boundaries and intimacy than someone who grew up as an only child. People who grew up having no clear sense of their own space and having to share everything sometimes grow up to become either compliant or defiant.

When we move into the adult world, we carry our learned experience about boundaries, intimacy, and closeness with us. Does being close mean that I can take your car without asking? Does it mean that I can go through your closets looking for something to wear? Does it mean that I can read your mail, answer your phone calls, interrupt your conversations, erase your e-mail, keep you awake at night with my radio, change the setting on your thermostat or air conditioning without asking, and generally deny you privacy? In short, where do I end and you begin? Boundaries have to do with knowing the difference between self and others. They have to do with knowing the difference between what belongs to "me," what belongs to "you," and what belongs to "us." We become most acutely aware of our boundaries when we feel that they are being invaded by someone who is failing to give our opinions, needs, and priorities the respect we feel they deserve.

Some people put up so many boundaries that they go through the world almost as though they are encapsulated in impenetrable shells. Floyd is one such person. Nobody ever asks him to volunteer his time for any project; nobody ever asks him to donate money; nobody ever borrows anything. His favorite word is "no." Another favorite is "no way." He has made it very clear to his family and friends that all he wants to do is sit in his den and watch television; he resents most attempts at conversation as intrusions. Although he has been married for twenty years, his wife still doesn't know how much money he earns.

Other people appear to be almost without protective boundaries. Ellie, for example, is everybody's best friend. Her door is wide open to anybody she meets, and dozens of people regularly take advantage of her inability to say no. She babysits other people's kids and pets; she provides limitless home-cooked meals; she loans money to just about anybody who asks. Ellie is completely open about her feelings and hides nothing.

Floyd's boundaries are so powerful that they border on the impenetrable, while Ellie has so few boundaries that she runs the risk of becoming a human doormat. Guess which of these people a narcissist would find most attractive? Okay, so that question is a no-brainer. It's easy to see that narcissists would avoid Floyd like the plague because they would have no place to attach or spin their illusion.

Like Ellie, some of us have had our boundaries crossed so many times in so many ways that by the time we're in our twenties, we've developed such an extreme level of flexibility that it borders on being unhealthy. We're the people narcissists find most attractive. Our boundaries are fuzzy. We may have had parents who were withholding or who shut us out. Because of this we may have become desensitized to people with impenetrable boundaries; we're accustomed to not being prioritized and receiving little attention. At the same time, because we have no strong boundaries of our own, we are too quickly apt to fall into someone else's merger fantasies. This makes us particularly vulnerable to narcissists.

A Clear Sense of Self = A Clear Sense of Boundaries

Think about how you would react in the following situation:

You're sitting in an office working on an important project that interests you. The door is closed. A coworker, let's call her Angie, opens the door and sticks her head in. "Do you have a second?" she asks.

What do you answer?

Well, if you answered no, Angie would probably go away, and you wouldn't be troubled any further.

But let's assume you answered yes. Let's assume that you don't like saying no. You may have thought to yourself, doesn't everybody have "a second?" So Angie comes into your office and begins to tell you her story, which involves a disagreement that she had with a sales clerk in a shopping mall. While what she has to say is important to Angie, it's not all that important in the greater scheme of things. In fact, even Angie will probably forget about it in a few days. But as Angie's story unfolds, one second becomes five minutes and then ten. Angie's story seems to have no end point in sight. She is totally wrapped up in her own head and her own story. Nothing else is important to her.

What do you do?

Do you try to send signs that convey that you want to go back to what you were doing? Do you shuffle papers? Look at the clock? Do you start to become agitated or uncomfortable? Do you say anything? Do you try to make a joke about Angie's concept of time? Do you get so internally upset that you feel your blood pressure rising?

How long do you wait before you speak up? Do you ever speak up?

How about this question: are you the kind of person who might actually put your own work aside and turn your time and attention totally over to Angie and her monologue? Perhaps when you do this you tell yourself that you can do your own work later because Angie seems to really need to talk, and you really want to be a good and kind person.

No matter how great the degree of your responsiveness to Angie's interruption, one thing is true. When you allowed Angie's low-level crisis to become more important than your own work project, you conveyed a message: you let Angie know that it was very easy to get around your boundaries. Angie now realizes that you are somebody on whose door she can always knock. This is how the Angies of this world take advantage of your good nature. This is how you invite narcissists to take over your life.

We understand that there is a difference between a self-involved coworker who creates a minor disturbance in your life and a romantic partner who creates total chaos. But the dynamic that allows a coworker to invade your space or a neighbor to bend your ear is the same one that allows a romantic partner to become so all-important that you and your needs are forgotten. The minute you decided to look up from your important project to listen to Angie complain about her shopping mishaps, you sent out a loud signal that said you and/or your work have less of a priority than a coworker's need to vent.

We know what your argument to this is going to be. You are going to say, "No, my first priority is to be a kind and helpful person." And we respect that and agree with it. But we think you can be a good person and still let your work and your life assume a priority. We also think that the time you save by not letting people invade your emotional, mental, psychic, and physical space can be better spent on some genuine work to help others. Instead of listening to the Angies of this world, for example, you could devote some time volunteering. Big Brothers and Big Sisters always need volunteers. So do many other worthwhile organizations and charities. You could get involved with a project tutoring kids or helping people learn to read. Think about it: there are gazillions of ways to be a good person and help others without allowing selfish and self-serving narcissists to monopolize your time and your energy.

Your Boundaries Tell People That You Expect Respect

This is an important thing to remember: it's easier to establish and maintain reasonable boundaries if you know who you are, what you will and won't do, and what you expect from others. Think about the Popeye sentence "I yam what I yam." Can you be that clear about who you are?

You start out protecting yourself from narcissists by placing a real priority on your time, your energy, your plans, your commitments, and your values. Think about what you value. That's where you should be putting your energy and your focus. Being very clear about who you are and what you want from life makes it much harder for a narcissist to take advantage of you.

Do you have a clear sense of who you are? Do you have a clear sense of your values? Before you answer yes, ask yourself the following question: does the person you love exemplify those values? Let's take Logan, for example. He is totally responsible, honest, and trustworthy. These are qualities that he values. Yet his last two girlfriends have been both flaky and dishonest. How does this happen? Logan would say, "Hey, I didn't know what these women were like when I started to go out with them. Besides, I didn't pursue those women; they chased me." We would say, "Precisely."

If you are going to protect yourself from narcissists, it's really essential that you clearly express what you value and you avoid people and situations that don't reflect those values. Don't be afraid to state who you are and what values you hope to represent in life. People will respect you for it. People who grew up in an earlier age were accustomed to having their parents say, "If you want respect, you've gotta respect yourself." It's still true.

The men and women who are most likely to have narcissists take advantage of them haven't taken the time to formulate clear cut-goals about what they want to accomplish in life. Nurturing a sense of purpose and formulating goals that are not dependent on another person is one way to start to create boundaries in your life. And don't think simply because you and your partner have been involved for months or years that it is too late to state your values and create some boundaries that deserve respect.

Boundaries Are Your Primary Form of Protection Against Narcissists

Protecting your own boundaries shows those who lack boundaries what it means to have boundaries. You can't make other people create boundaries for themselves, but you can show somebody what it means to respect *yours*.

Without realizing it, people have boundary dialogues all day long. Take our friend Miranda. She's a real-estate agent in a small New England town. The people she's dealing with are the people she will be dealing with for the rest of her life, so she doesn't want to alienate anyone. Yet buyers and sellers who are anxious about housing concerns rarely exhibit any interest in protecting her right to private time, dinner time, weekend time, relaxation time. They call her at home at all kinds of crazy hours. Clients never seem to think about whether she could be preparing dinner for her two small children or doing anything else, for that matter. Now Miranda could deal with this by getting an unlisted number or she could screen all her calls or she could get another line. But she lives in a small town where open doors are the rule rather than the exception. Besides, she wants her kids, family, and friends to be able to reach her.

Miranda has learned to answer the phone in such a way that people quickly get the idea that Miranda has a life. Typically when a client calls her at home she says something like, "Hi Ron, I really want to talk to you, but I'm having dinner with my husband right now. Let me call you from the office first thing tomorrow morning." She keeps her tone and her voice pleasant but firm. The message Miranda conveys to her caller is, You are important to me, but I am important to me too, and I have a life. She is telling her callers something, and she is teaching them something.

Miranda never says anything like, "Do you know what time it is?" or "I can't believe you're calling me at 10 P.M.!" That would make the callers defensive. Miranda doesn't want to make her callers annoyed or angry. She wants to educate them in a way that doesn't make them feel accused or wrong or bad. We can all take a lesson from Miranda and learn some sentences that will work in our own lives.

People who are involved with narcissists need to learn to say no, but they also need to learn to do it in a way that doesn't create more anger and excessive strife, chaos, or confusion in their own lives. In our own lives, we have found that it is helpful if you say something positive first, and then draw the boundary line.

Cassandra recently started going out with a guy who called every night at 11 P.M. and then wanted to talk for an hour or more. Cassandra has a demanding job and two kids that have to get to school every morning. Here's a boundary Cassandra drew. She said, "I love talking to you. Everything I find out about you makes me like you more, but if I'm going to continue to hold my job, I have to be in bed early on weeknights. I know I can say this to you and you'll understand. But you're not the only person who calls late at night, so I'm going to turn off my phone at 10:30."

Here are some examples of other boundary sentences that can be used at the beginning of a relationship.

- "I like you a lot, but I don't know you well enough to go home with you. Why don't you call me in the next couple of days and we can make plans to get together and find out more about each other."

- "I think you are the smartest/most exciting/most wonderful/etc. man/woman I've ever met, but I think we should know each other at least six months before we start making plans to move in together or spend the rest of our lives together."

- "I know and appreciate how busy you are, but I am terribly busy, too, so if you are ever more than fifteen minutes late, I am going to assume that our plans have changed, and I'm going to go on to my next activity/appointment/plan, etc."

- "I think you are just great, but when I think about the kind of relationship I want, I always envision being with someone who is going to want me to be an integral part of his/her life. If you don't want to have that kind of relationship, I'm going to have to try to find that kind of partner. We can always be friends."

Introducing New Boundaries in the Middle of an Ongoing Relationship

Obviously it's easier if you begin all your relationships by being clear about your boundaries. It's also obvious that if you haven't done this and are already in the middle of a troubled relationship, you are going to have a much harder time establishing your reasonable boundaries.

Before you try to introduce new boundaries in your relationship, make a list of things that are most important to you in a relationship. List your major priorities and values. Start by listing eight to ten items that are important to you, and then pick two or three on which you might want to focus.

Here are some of the things that might appear on your list:

- "It's very important to me that my partner be kind to my children."
- "It's very important to me that my partner not talk to me in a sarcastic and angry tone of voice."
- "It's very important to me that my partner supports my creativity."
- "It's very important to me that my partner supports my goals."
- "It's very important to me that my partner stop spending our money on alcohol/drugs/gambling."
- "It's very important to me that my partner is monogamous."
- "It's very important to me that my partner respect my spiritual or religious values."
- "It's very important to me that my partner respect my relationship with my family and other people."
- "It's very important to me that my partner not say or do anything that embarrasses me in front of my friends or family."
- "It's very important to me that my partner respects my work and does not interfere in my work relationships."
- "It's very important to me that my partner not be jealous of everything I do and/or everybody I know."

After you have your list, choose one that has a high priority to you and your relationship and see if you can create a boundary sentence for it. Our friend Patti recently drew a boundary for her husband, Shel, who has a drinking problem. She said, "Shel, I love you very much, and I want you to be happy, but it's also important that the children and I be happy. I've decided something; I am not buying liquor any more. If you want to drink, you are going to have to do it without my help." Patti said this when she was in a good mood and when she was in the process of cutting Shel a piece of chocolate cake. She didn't want to start a fight; she just wanted to get her point across. When Shel said, "What are you blabbering about now?" Patti smiled sweetly and said, "I'm just letting you know my position." And she is sticking to it.

Here are examples of some other boundary sentences:

- "I think you are just the best looking/cutest/most handsome/prettiest person in the room, but if you don't stop flirting with everybody at this party, I'm going to have to go home now because I find it disrespectful to me."

- "I really understand how hard you work and how tired you are, but I work hard, too. If it's too much for you to support my priority of having a neat home and pick up all those wet towels and your clothes, all I'm going to be able to do is pile everything together in the basement until you can get around to it."

- "I really appreciate how great you look in the clothes you buy and how attractive you keep the house with all the stuff you put in it, and how fabulous the car looks with the weekly waxing, but I can't afford to pay for all this, so I am putting all my money in a separate checking account and closing down all the joint credit cards."

Being Firm About Your Boundary Sentences

The cardinal rule supporting the creation of boundaries is this: you have to be prepared to back up whatever you say. This is why you can never, ever put down a boundary until you know you are 100 percent ready to do what you say. Jeb, for example, told his girlfriend that he wasn't going to spend more than fifteen minutes waiting for her any more. Then, last week, as he stood in front of a movie theatre and his girlfriend was nowhere in sight, Jeb discovered that he was unable to walk away. He says that he was too worried about where she could be. He also worried that she would be really angry. Besides, it was raining, and he "didn't want her to get wet."

Jeb discovered how difficult it is to make his boundary sentence stick. He was so stuck with the old patterns of how he and his girlfriend relate to each other that he couldn't break out of those old ways. People who are involved with narcissists are often afraid to create new boundaries. Here are some of the things they worry about.

• If I'm not there, doing what I always do, something terrible could happen to him/her.

• If I'm not there, doing what I always do, he/she could get drunk/do drugs/get into trouble.

• If I'm not there, doing what I always do, he/she could find somebody else or forget about me.

• If I'm not there doing what I always do, he/she could get angry enough to leave me.

• If I'm not there doing what I always do, he/she might learn that I'm not really indispensable.

• If I'm not there doing what I always do, he/she might do something terrible to get even.

Let's acknowledge it: the primary reason we don't state new boundaries and stick to them is because we are scared of the consequences. Working out some new boundaries and finding ways to make them stick are examples of skills and benefits to be gained from personal counseling.

SUGGESTION: DON'T TAKE HIS/HER BAD BEHAVIOR PERSONALLY

Kimberly has some advice for all of us. She says:

"My boyfriend and I just broke up. This is not the first time we broke up, but I think it will be the last. I broke up with him for the same reason that I always break up with him. He says and does things that are so vicious and insensitive that I would be embarrassed to tell anybody about them. When he speaks to me sometimes, his tone of voice can be completely disgusting. I wouldn't talk to anybody the way he talks to me.

I always go back to him because he sweet talks me into doing so. I love him when he's nice to me. I hate him when he's mean. After ten years of going back with him, I think I've learned some stuff about his personality. Some of it is painful for me to face. I guess this is the bottom line: I realize that I don't really matter. When he's nice to me, it has nothing to do with me. And when he's disgusting to me, it has nothing to do with me. People were always telling me not to take it personally when he was mean to me. But now I see that I shouldn't take any of it personally—not even the good part. He's just a guy who doesn't know the first thing about love, and I'm just the girl he stumbled upon. It didn't have to be me who got involved with him; it could have been anybody who paid attention to him. I have to stop taking anything he does personally."

Kimberly is sharing some very good advice. Many of us have been told not to take another person's negative behavior personally: "Don't take it personally; it's just the way he/she is." Haven't we all heard that? But has it ever been suggested to you that you shouldn't take another person's positive behavior personally? Don't we all want to believe that when we meet somebody who showers us with intensity and passion, that it has to do with who we are?

It's very, very painful to face the idea that a narcissist's protestations of love and romance may have more to do with his/her MO than it does with what he/she is feeling for us. It's even very painful to face the idea that when a narcissist gets angry at us, it has more to do with his/her inner problems than it does with us. It can make you and the relationship seem meaningless, which can hurt a lot. However, when we begin not to take it personally, we get perspective on what's going on.

This is not to say that there isn't a connection between you and your narcissistic partner, because there undoubtedly is. However, all those spectacular highs and all those miserable lows are coming from a part of your partner's psyche that really isn't connected to anybody else. It's melodrama without any depth. This is an important point to remember when you're tying to have a relationship with a narcissist. We've said this before, but we'll say it again: narcissists are renowned for shallow emotions. Think about what it means to have shallow emotions. This means that your narcissistic partner can be sobbing in your arms one minute and dancing the fandango with a perfect stranger the next.

NARCISSISTS DISPLAY EMOTIONS THAT CANNOT BE TRUSTED!

When narcissists talk about love, they don't mean the same thing that the rest of us mean. When they act annoyed or angry, it doesn't necessarily have anything to do with anything that you are or are not doing.

Let's take an example of infidelity: Ryan and Tessa just spent an idyllic weekend in the mountains. When they come home, Tessa is on cloud nine because of everything that took place between them. On Wednesday, Tessa discovers that Ryan is out with another woman. She doesn't understand it; she can't comprehend Ryan's logic. She assumes that infidelity only occurs when people are unhappy in their relationships or reacting to something their partners are doing. She assumes that people are unfaithful because their partners are being unkind or withholding; she thinks they are being unfaithful because they are trying in some way "to get even." Tessa is sure this is not the case with Ryan. Tessa has to understand that Ryan is a narcissist. His infidelity has nothing whatsoever to do with Tessa. It has everything to do with who Ryan is. That's why people tell Tessa not to take it personally.

We quickly want to assure readers that we are not suggesting that they learn to tolerate infidelity. We absolutely think that fidelity is an essential ingredient in a successful relationship. We do want readers to understand, however, that narcissists have shallow and untrustworthy emotions; we do want readers to understand that narcissistic behavior exists almost as though it is in a vacuum. You are not creating it, and you cannot cure it. So, as we said, don't take it personally.

SUGGESTION: UNDERSTAND HOW YOU "FEED" THE NARCISSISTS IN YOUR LIFE

Anyone who has ever seen *The Little Shop of Horrors* remembers the plant that kept hollering "Feed ME!" Do you remember that plant? It looked so appealing, but underneath its cute green exterior lived a bloodthirsty megalomaniac who wanted to take over the world. The plant started out small and insignificant looking, but as people catered to its demands, the plant puffed up and became an out-of-control monster who wanted more and more.

Living with narcissists is like living with that plant. They cry out for emotional feeding and require constant attention. "Narcissistic supply" is the all-encompassing general term that we've seen used a lot recently to describe the emotional and psychic nourishment that narcissists require on a daily basis. If we cater to a narcissist's hunger for anything, from attention to sex, we are the ones who are providing narcissistic supply. We pay attention to what the narcissists in our lives say they need because we love them, but often when we do this we merely reinforce their most toxic qualities. We become accomplices.

Narcissistic supply describes all the things that narcissists feed on. People who are most critical of narcissists say that anyone who regularly nourishes a narcissist's needs is a source of narcissistic supply. For example, let's say you love your partner; because of that, you especially love having sex with him/her. Sex then becomes a way of getting closer and more intimate. A narcissist, on the other hand, sees sex primarily as a way of establishing power and dominance and showing off his/her attractiveness or seductive skills. Sex thus becomes a source of narcissistic supply.

Anyone who has ever had a relationship with a narcissist knows how easy it is to become the person giving and giving and giving without end. When this happens, we are feeding the narcissist, much as Seymour, the hero of *Little Shop of Horrors*, fed the monstrous green plant. Ask yourself whether you have become an accomplice in your relationship with your partner. Is what you are giving your partner, in terms of love and support, helping him/her evolve into someone who is even more selfish? Like the malignant potted plant, toxic narcissists tend to take advantage of the people who "feed" and nurture them regularly. This is an important principle to keep in mind. Many people who are involved with narcissists believe that if they continue on a path of endless giving, eventually the narcissist will come to his/her senses. We think the chances of this approach working are next to zilch. Sometimes we give to narcissists because we like having an important role and we encourage their dependency. Eventually this will probably backfire.

SUGGESTION: REFUSE TO PLAY THE BLAME GAME

One of the least-effective ways of dealing with someone with narcissistic tendencies is to try to assign blame of any kind. Remember that narcissists want to feel superior and hate to feel inferior. They don't ever want to feel that they did anything wrong. When two people are having a relationship, of course, millions of things can go wrong. Let's just take a situation in which somebody forgot to lock the front door. You notice it in the morning and you say, in what you think is an innocuous tone of voice, "No harm done, but you forgot to lock the front door when you came in last night." Many narcissists lack a sense of proportion and will not allow that kind of comment to slide. In fact, there is a very good chance that they will mentally start thinking about all the various ways in which you might have made small errors or missteps. Narcissists often say or do things to make sure their partners feel inferior or lacking so that they can feel superior. That's one of the ways they maintain their sense of superiority.

Narcissists love to put others down. Remember all the tactics narcissists use to feel puffed up; don't open the door to dialogues of the "It's your fault"/"No, it's your fault" variety. If at all possible, try not to introduce blame or start arguments about any of the small things that we all do in the course of living. It can initiate an ongoing and never-ending competition.

Instead of blaming, try to find ways of speaking up for

yourself without indicting your partner. For example: You and your partner are planning to go to a movie. He comes home and says, let's see *Planet of the Numbskulls*. Instead of saying, "Why do we always have to go to the movies you want," try saying, "Maybe we could see that next week, because I was really counting on seeing something else." Then name the movie you want to see. Try to maintain a positive, constructive tone.

SUGGESTION: REMEMBER THAT YOUR PARTNER IS AN ADULT

Liz always tried to protect her partner. She says, "I saw Mike as a lonely child who had been hurt by life. I thought it was my job to protect him and make sure that nothing ever upset him. Once he got an ugly old stain on his favorite jacket, and it wouldn't come out. I devoted myself to shopping in stores and on the Internet trying to duplicate the jacket so he wouldn't be upset. I just didn't want him to be unhappy about anything."

Liz's attitude toward her partner is not all that unusual. People who fall in love with narcissists often end up viewing them as vulnerable children who need their protection. Once again, most of the people we spoke to said that this was a big mistake and that this attitude did little to help establish the kind of relationship they wanted.

There are lots of other ways in which you might fail to treat your narcissistic partner as an adult. Ask yourself: Do you make excuses for your partner? Do you cover for your partner's mistakes? Do you run interference for your partner with other people? Do you go out of your way to protect your partner, much as you would with a child?

Treating your partner as you would a child is not good for your partner; it's not good for your relationship; and it's not good for you. The best advice we can give you is to try to let go of this attitude.

SUGGESTION: DON'T EXPECT YOUR EMOTIONAL RESPONSES TO INFLUENCE A NARCISSIST

Vanessa thought that if she got really upset, her feelings would take priority and her boyfriend would stop hurting her. She was wrong. She says, "The other day Chris got me so upset that I couldn't stop crying. When I say couldn't stop, I mean couldn't stop. I think in the back of my head I always believed that if I got really upset, Chris would be sympathetic. I was wrong. He just got angry. The harder I cried, the angrier he got. Finally he stormed out the door. I was just sitting there sobbing."

Repeat after us: *Narcissists are not capable of empathy. Narcissists are not capable of empathy.*

Narcissists do not and cannot feel what you feel. They are not going to be responsive to emotional appeals. Many narcissists are experts at tuning out another person's emotionality. When you become emotional, they can't handle it. In fact, they may think your tears are a ploy.

Sometimes they may simply become more emotional than you are. If you cry, your significant other could cry louder—no matter what the underlying situation or dynamic is. Over the years, many men and women have told us about being brutally rejected by narcissists under perfectly horrible circumstances. They didn't even get the opportunity to react because their narcissistic partners were crying so hard that there was no room for anyone else to get upset. Kathy, for example, says that when the man she was living with decided that he had fallen in love with somebody else, he came home and told Kathy that she had to leave the apartment they shared and for which they had jointly bought furniture because he couldn't handle it. He was sobbing uncontrollably when he told her that he couldn't bear being around her because he was so upset. He then sobbed for two straight hours as he helped a shell-shocked Kathy pack her things. Finally, still crying, he put her and her belongings into a cab headed for her sister's. Whenever Kathy tried to say anything, he cried even louder and talked about "the pain" he was feeling.

The point of all this is that if you expect to have a serious conversation with a narcissist, you have to handle it like a business negotiation. Be calm, be collected, have clear, nonemotional arguments prepared. Get a friend to role-play with you. Say what you want to say in an even-tempered, nonconfrontational way. Use positive, non-blaming sentences. Don't say things that you think will make your narcissistic partner guilty; it won't work. Chances are that all he/she will do is get angry.

SUGGESTION: STOP BEING SO UNDERSTANDING OF NARCISSISTS

We know that if you're a decent human being, you can't help having feelings.

This is true, but when it comes to a narcissistic partner, you can try to be aware and keep those feelings more in check. Stop feeling what you think he/she feels. Stop thinking what you think he/she thinks. Stop being so sensitive to his/her pain. Not that long ago, Julia was talking to a woman named Brigid whose narcissistic boyfriend had rejected her. Within weeks of the breakup, the ex-boyfriend met and married someone else. Within a couple of months after the marriage, the ex-boyfriend began once again to call Brigid, saying that his wife didn't really love him the way Brigid had, and that while he didn't want to divorce his wife, he also wanted to see Brigid.

Brigid told Julia that she had come to terms with the end of the relationship and in some ways was relieved, because this boyfriend had been so bad for her. Nonetheless, Brigid said that she was still upset and started crying. When Julia asked what specifically had triggered her tears, Brigid said, "I just feel so bad for him. I know he painted himself into a total corner. He sounded frantic. I'm worried that he's going to get sick."

We think it's important that you not fall into the trap of

allowing yourself to become consumed with what you think your partner is experiencing. When you do this, you demonstrate that you are also not clear on the difference between self and other. Instead of worrying about what your partner may or may not be feeling, pay some attention to what *you* are feeling.

SUGGESTION: STOP TRYING TO WIN POPULARITY CONTESTS.

You do not have to be the "nicest" person in the room. Remember that 1) narcissists are amazingly demanding, and 2) people who fall in love with narcissists tend to want to please their partners' demands. In fact, people who fall in love with narcissists are usually the kind of people who want to make everyone happy.

Keep in mind that a relationship is not a popularity contest. Stop trying to win a congeniality award. Your eagerness to please sends narcissists the message that you are somebody who is easily manipulated and that your good intentions can be misused. Give a reasonable and appropriate amount, but no more. Don't always be the person who "doesn't mind" doing the extra work. Don't always be the person who is racing around catering to your partner's needs and wants. Too much giving is often the product of an incredibly open-handed and open-hearted approach to life. This can be a lovely quality, but not if you consistently put yourself in a position where your good intentions and your good heart are misused. Once again, this brings us back to boundaries and the need to be a little more self-protective when dealing with narcissists.

Learn how to say things like, "While you're up, could you please put this in the refrigerator." "Could you please pick up milk while you're on the way home?" "It's your turn to take out the garbage honey." **Don't always be the one who does everything!**

If your partner is accustomed to a dynamic in which you do all the work, don't expect this to change overnight. But you can make some small inroads a little at a time, and the results can be worth the effort.

SUGGESTION: BE MORE SELF-PROTECTIVE AND LESS VULNERABLE

Did you ever consider that you might be *too* vulnerable? Did you ever think that you might be *too* sensitive? Just as they are often too giving, men and women who love narcissists tend to be extremely sensitive and easily hurt. If you are attempting to maintain a relationship with a narcissist, you might want to try to grow a slightly tougher skin so that you can step back and get some perspective on what is taking place. You may be thinking that your vulnerability and sensitivity are good qualities that should be cherished. We agree. That's why we think you would be best served by saving them for someone who appreciates them. A narcissist may pay lip service to your decency, honesty, and vulnerability, but that doesn't mean that he/she is going to treat you as though these are precious qualities to be protected.

Narcissists can be demeaning, negative, hurtful, sarcastic, and incredibly insensitive to anything except their own "pain." Keep that in mind the next time your partner does or says something hurtful. Instead of crying or feeling hurt and distraught, step back and count to ten. Get some perspective on what is taking place. We're not being sarcastic or dismissive of your feelings when we tell you to step back. What we're trying to do is suggest ways that you stop pouring good energy into a negative scenario. The problem with expressing your upset to your partner is that if he/she doesn't respond appropriately, you become even more hurt. All of your energy then goes into this perfectly rotten situation. If you begin to remove yourself emotionally even a little at a time, you may begin to get a better sense of perspective. You may find that you are hurting less and less and needing less and less from this person. This is a good thing, so don't let it scare you.

SUGGESTION: CHANGE YOUR EXPECTATIONS

If you want to have a relationship with a narcissist, you may well have to change your idea of what it is you expect from a relationship. You are dealing with someone who is limited in all the ways we have discussed. We know that what you want is to have the idyllic relationship you thought was possible when you first met your partner. Ask yourself whether you feel that, at this point, this is a realistic wish.

What you could do for at least a short period of time is give yourself a break and just try to accept your partner with all his/her limitations and flaws. (The exception to this, of course, is physical abuse, which cannot and should not be accepted.) Instead of trying to change your partner's selfish ways, give up all pleading, cajoling, complaining, and arguing. Just realize and accept that this approach is not going to work. Take a look at your partner realistically and accept what you see, whatever that is. Start by trying this approach for a week. Instead of putting your mental energy into what your partner isn't giving you, put your focus and energy on doing things for yourself.

Change the way you think. Don't expect that your partner or your relationship is going to change your life for the better. Take back that power for yourself. See if you can find ways to make improvements all on your own. Do something for yourself. It doesn't matter if you decide to take a course or take a walk. Making decisions for yourself by yourself is an empowering and liberating experience.

SUGGESTION: KEEP REMINDING YOURSELF THAT REALITY IS YOUR FRIEND

Once again, all relationships with narcissists tend to be fraught with fantasy and illusion. If you're going to maintain your equilibrium, you have to keep those tootsies firmly on terra firma. It's enough that your partner is filled with fantasies without adding your own. Realistically, be aware of your limitations. Let go of your healing fantasies; let go of your fantasies about being able to change what others cannot.

Look at your situation. Look at the tactics you have used that have already failed. Don't keep stepping on the same minefields. Stay calm and realistic, and whatever you do, don't add even more drama to your relationship.

SUGGESTION: DON'T BE EMBARRASSED TO ADMIT THAT YOUR SITUATION REQUIRES PROFESSIONAL HELP

We'd like to remind you that negotiating a relationship with a narcissist is no piece of cake. The best thing you can do for yourself is to get professional help. Many people try to convince their partners to go into some form of couples counseling. This is certainly worth a try. If your partner, however, adamantly refuses, don't give up on the idea of counseling. Do it for yourself. What knowledge you gain for yourself will help you and may help the relationship as well. If you can't afford therapy, see what kinds of social services are available in your state. There are amazing resources that are available, particularly for families.

Thirteen

NARCISSISTIC AND COMMITMENTPHOBIC

YOU WILL REMEMBER THAT NARCISSISTS HAVE A tendency to judge themselves in an extreme "I am the best!" or "I am the worst!" fashion. The more extreme the narcissism, the more extreme the conflicting views of self. So what happens when toxic narcissists get involved in romantic relationships? How do they judge their partners? It's not going to be a surprise to hear that narcissists are equally conflicted in the way they look at the people in their lives, particularly those who are closest. Their attitudes toward romantic partners can flip- flop in an instant.

When Samantha, for example, met Nicholas, she couldn't get over how much he seemed to like her. He liked her taste in clothes, food, and furniture. He shared her opinions on books, music, movies, and friends. He was simpatico with her views on politics and spirituality. He told her that he couldn't get over the fact that he had met a woman who shared so many of his interests and attitudes. He told her she was beautiful. He bought her presents. He bought her a ring. He said that making her happy was the most important thing in his life. When he met Samantha's best friend Kaylee, he put his arm around Samantha and said, "Do you know how much I adore this woman?"

"Wow," Kaylee said later to Samantha, "He seems gaga over you."

This lasted until the day they moved in together. Within twenty-four hours, Nicholas began to express dozens of negative opinions about things Samantha did. Why did she, for example, sit with her legs tucked under her on the couch? It made her look fatter than she was. It was also hard on the furniture. Why did she leave the spoon she used to stir her coffee on the kitchen counter? It was disgusting and made him want to throw up. Why did she wear her red dress to dinner with his friends? It made her look trampy.

After they moved in together, Nicholas was less eager to spend time with her; he was also less romantic. Walking down the street, Samantha saw him openly staring at other women. They went to the theater one night, and as soon as Samantha began to talk about how much she liked the performances, Nicholas became very sarcastic and condescending of her opinions. They went to a party; Nicholas ignored her and flirted with another woman. When she told him that she found his behavior hurtful, he said, "Well, get used to it." It was a shock to her. She had looked forward to living with Nicholas because they shared so much. But now he was acting as though they had little in common; in fact, sometimes he acted as though she was the enemy. Before they moved in together, Nicholas had been pushing to get married immediately. Now, he didn't even want to buy a dining-room table together; he said he thought they should wait before they did anything so permanent.

Samantha was stunned. One of the primary reasons she found Nicholas so wonderful was that he seemed to have fallen head over heels in love with her. He had called her the center of his universe. What was going on?

Was Nicholas withdrawing because he had gotten too close too fast? Was he reacting to more intimacy than he could handle? What was going on? Was Nicholas exhibiting signs of commitmentphobia? And what does that mean?

WE THINK THAT THE WORST-CASE COMMITMENT-PHOBICS ARE OFTEN TOXIC NARCISSISTS

We'd like to start by saying two things: a) not *all* narcissists are commitmentphobic, and b) not *all* commitmentphobics are narcissistic. However, we've been interviewing people about their relationships for many years now, and the connection between commitmentphobia and narcissism is one we couldn't help but notice. A vast number of the people who have written to us about their commitmentphobic partners have described behavior that is blatantly narcissistic.

This connection is not surprising. Men and women with strong narcissistic issues are almost inevitably ambivalent about relationships. They may want to experience intimacy and togetherness, but they typically lack solid, loving role models and are inexperienced in knowing how to love. Their childhood wounds have often left them fearful and believing that intimacy is dangerous; they are afraid to lower their defenses and trust another human being. The worst part of this is that many of them are so defended against their early injuries that they don't even know how afraid they are. Let this be a warning to those of you who think you can teach them how to love. These people don't think they have a problem. They think *you* are the problem. Small wonder that so many narcissists act out in commitmentphobic ways.

It's been almost twenty years since we coined the term *commitmentphobia* to describe people with an almost paralyzing and phobic fear of intimacy. People who have read our two books about commitmentphobia—*Men Who Can't Love* and *He's Scared, She's Scared*—know that when we talk about commitmentphobic relationships and commitmentphobic romantic partners, we are not describing men and women who are a little bit nervous about getting married. We are talking about relationships that evolve in a very specific pattern; we are talking about romantic partners who behave in very hurtful and predictable ways. The relationship we describe as commitmentphobic has several defining characteristics. We break it down into four separate stages:

The Beginning: All the commitmentphobic partner can think about is how much he/she wants you.

The Middle: Your commitmentphobic partner has made the sale. You are in love. But no sooner do you give your heart before your partner begins to get scared and start to withdraw.

The End: Your partner is running away, and you are doing everything you can to get back to the beginning.

The Bitter End: It's over, and you are as heartbroken as you are confused.

In our first book about commitmentphobia, we concentrated on men, because it seemed to us at the time that the pattern was primarily male. However, we very quickly began to be aware of the growing number of women who were also acting out in a similar pattern despite societal pressures and their biological clocks. In this regard it's interesting to note that for many years, psychologists believed that almost all narcissists were male, and even today, there is an assumption among some people that more men than women have the disorder. Our own conclusion is that commitmentphobic/narcissistic partners can be male or female, but just as there are differences in traditional male/female roles, there will certainly be some differences in how men and women with commitmentphobic/narcissistic issues behave.

Here is a brief summary of what we mean when we talk about a commitmentphobic relationship.

THE BEGINNING OF THE COMMITMENTPHOBIC RELATIONSHIP

The first stage of the commitmentphobic relationship is advanced and driven by the fearful partner, who at this stage, is acting out a fantasy and showing no ambivalence and no fear. If you are the person who is being pursued, you are seen as the idealized love object. During this beginning phase, the fantasy-driven commitmentphobic partner (CP) is doing everything possible to convince you that you are the one. He or she is in hot pursuit and trying to impress you with his/her best qualities, skills, talents, and techniques; yes, he/she may appear troubled and/or insecure, but this is offset by intensity, passion, sensitivity, and the appearance of emotional vulnerability.

In the meantime, your role is that of the idealized love object who can do no wrong. You are the recipient of warm and fuzzy e-mails, phone calls, love notes, and sometimes even poetry; you receive gifts and compliments. The CP refers to activities the two of you will share and gives you the impression that you are building a future together. He/she implies that no matter what went wrong in previous relationships, it will be different with you.

You may be reluctant to allow this person into your life, but eventually you succumb to the flattery and the seduction. Someone appears to have seen you for who you are and has fallen in love with you for all the right reasons! How could you not be persuaded? It is as though this person has a key to your soul; it can be like a dream come true. For a moment, you feel truly loved and understood.

The beginning of a commitmentphobic relationship can last an hour, a week, a month, or a year; how long it lasts is completely dependent on how long it takes for you to respond to the CP and open your heart.

THE MIDDLE STAGE OF A COMMITMENTPHOBIC RELATIONSHIP

Your partner realizes that you have been won over. Almost immediately there is a sea change in the relationship. As soon as you make a commitment, your partner begins to feel conflicted and starts to notice ways in which you are not his or her idealized fantasy. It may start with something very small. *Very small.* A little flaw in your diction. A problem with your choice of shoes. That's how it tends to start; something so small that you might not notice if it weren't for the fact that it seems peculiarly out of context given the elevated position that you thought you occupied. But it starts. And it builds. Sometimes so fast that your head is reeling from the change.

Now that the conquest is made, the CP's conflicts emerge. He/she may withdraw emotionally; he/she may begin to have anxiety attacks. Typically the CP reacts to his/her conflicts by creating problems and distance within the relationship. Sometimes he/she begins to find fault with you; sometimes he/she begins to erect peculiar boundaries. He/she may do things to make you feel excluded from his/her life. Your CP may start to act annoyed or look for excuses not to see you. It is so different from what it was at the beginning that you are taken by surprise and don't know how to react. Typically, by now, you have bought into the fantasies that were part and parcel of the beginning of the relationship. Your CP convinced you that you were a couple. Using the CP's words and promises as your anchor, you try to follow through accordingly; you try to be more loving, giving, and understanding, which inevitably doesn't work.

Instead of following through on the plans you made, the CP is backing off. There is often a break or change in the sexual relationship; your ardent lover seems withdrawn. You may become aware that he/she is flirting with someone else. Through it all, he/she is giving you double messages and mixed signals. You are caught in the middle of a push-pull dynamic. On the one hand, you are sure that he/she still has strong feelings for you. On the other, you feel rejected and hurt. Despite the romantic, fantasy-like beginning, you are no longer the priority you once were. You are also confused because you feel that this person is also hurting, and you don't know what to do. You are probably asking what is wrong, and you may be issuing or thinking about issuing an ultimatum. In the meantime, the CP may be promising you that everything will be okay.

The middle of a commitmentphobic relationship can last for a week or for a lifetime. Some couples go through this kind of back-and-forth dance for a lifetime. When this happens, there is usually a pattern fraught with ultimatums, promises to change, breakups, promises to change, ultimatums, promises to change, never-ending drama, and a terrible amount of emotional suffering.

THE END OF THE COMMITMENTPHOBIC RELATIONSHIP

Both partners realize that they cannot continue this way; something has to happen. You feel that everything would be resolved if only your partner could make a real commitment. Your CP, on the other hand, is gearing up for full-flight mode. He/she may be thinking about a relationship with somebody else; he she may be withdrawing sexually; he/she may be telling you lies; he/she may have put up impossible boundaries; he/she may provoke arguments or fights. Typically the CP is refusing to do anything to improve your relationship.

Everything is so different from the way it was at the beginning of the relationship that you may still be having an impossible time processing what is going wrong. The relationship has gone from a dream come true to a topsy-turvy nightmare.

The end of a commitmentphobic relationship is often associated or precipitated by some special event. It could be a holiday, a vacation plan, a family wedding, or even an illness. Events such as these force the CP to make a choice. Does he/she want others to acknowledge that you are indeed a couple? If the CP is making you feel excluded, you might issue a final ultimatum. The CP feels forced to make a decision.

THE BITTER END OF A COMMITMENTPHOBIC RELATIONSHIP

The CP typically ends a relationship in one of three ways.

1. The CP provokes you into ending it by doing something totally unkind.

Think of all the terrible things that a romantic partner could do to make it impossible for you to continue. Does he/she ignore you? Does he/she begin or renew a romantic relationship with someone else? Does he/she treat you so badly that it's embarrassing to admit? It's as though you no longer have any power in the relationship whatsoever. This makes you feel sad, hurt, and humiliated. How could someone who seemed to care so much now care so little?

2. The CP withdraws slowly to the point where there is no relationship left.

At this point, the commitmentphobic partner often feels a strange combination of guilt and loss. He/she doesn't really have the courage to talk to you directly and leave the relationship; in fact, he/she may be just as confused as you are. To complicate matters, the CP often remains conflicted and doesn't want to lose you. This can be true even if he/she is involved with someone else.

3. The CP withdraws suddenly from your life—sometimes in very dramatic ways.

The Houdini approach is still used by some people as a way of ending a relationship. Over the years, dozens of men and women have told us about partners who went out to get cigarettes or milk and never returned. Sometimes the CP just stops calling. Sometimes the CP jumps into another relationship and uses this as a way of avoiding you. The CP doesn't want to hear your questions. He/she doesn't want to have to examine his/her own behavior.

However your commitmentphobic relationship ends, there is always the possibility of a curtain call during which your partner returns and brings back all the old relationship dynamics before jumping ship once more.

Typically, when a commitmentphobic relationship ends, not only are you deeply hurt and wounded, you are also totally confused. How could something that seemed so right go so wrong? Often you try to find reasons in something you did or said. You may spend hours and hours trying to analyze what went wrong. You may find it impossible to understand how this person who once presented himself or herself as your lover and protector could now treat you so badly. Two frequently asked questions are: How could he/she do this to me? and How could he/she do this to us? You may find it impossible to understand how somebody who once appeared so loving can now be so cruel.

COMMITMENTPHOBIA, NARCISSISM, AND FANTASY

When we first fall in love, most of us tend to see our partners in a rosy-pink glow. Then, as the relationship progresses, we begin to be more realistic about our mates. Ideally, we greet this reality with a certain amount of humor, understanding, and acceptance. Yes, when it comes to making money, George is no Donald Trump. But so what, he's a good guy, and you love him. Yes, Martha doesn't always look so hot in the morning, and sometimes she has a wicked case of PMS. But so what, she's a kind and loving woman, and most of the time she's very good to you.

Many of us start out searching for the perfect and ideal soul mate, and we bring with us a certain amount of fantasy. Then we fall in love and our relationships deepen and grow. The connection we share becomes less about the superficial elements that may have attracted us and more about the enduring qualities that deepen and enrich our lives. Our relationships become more and more real and we become less and less dependent on fantasy. This is good, this is natural, and this is necessary.

We all embark on our romantic relationships bringing with us a certain amount of fantasy. The fantasy is over when we realize that our partners are not perfect soul mates. That's when we settle down to the business of leading real lives with flesh-and- blood mates, who are individuals and not extensions of ourselves. Like us, our real-life partners are not perfect; these are real partners with whom we are not always in perfect accord. To lead real lives, we need to compromise, accommodate, and adjust our expections. Well, hear this: this is exactly what narcissists *don't* want to do. *Narcissists don't want to let go of their childlike fantasies.*

For a moment, let's go back to the myth of Narcissus. Remember that Narcissus didn't fall in love with himself; he fell in love with the image he saw reflected in the water, his mirror image. To some degree, isn't that all what we would like to have in a mate? Wouldn't it be easier if our partner was a mirror image who moves when we move, turns when we turn, and laughs when we laugh? Wouldn't it be wonderful if we were able to find partners who fulfilled all our fantasies? What a dream that would be: never to have to be alone and never to have to argue about which movie to see or how to set the thermostat.

People with narcissistic issues grew up with rich fantasies. These fantasies were often what allowed them to deal with a painful reality. Sometimes these fantasies were all they had. They grew up dreaming about the perfect partner who would one day love them the way they wanted to be loved, the partner who would take the place of the perfect mommy or daddy they didn't have. That partner would fill the void and make up for everything that had ever gone wrong in their lives. That person would be able to mirror them perfectly.

In short, narcissists want to recapture a feeling they never had. It's an unrealistic dream. When they meet new romantic partners, they idealize them until reality sets in. They have found partners who love them, but they still feel empty. They still feel the same. When that happens, they tend to assume that the fault is with the other person and not with themselves. *Hard-core narcissists will find something wrong with every person they meet.*

If you are in love with a narcissist who is withdrawing love and acceptance, you know how excruciatingly painful it can be. Because you still love, admire, and trust this person, you are deeply affected by the negativity. Instead of thinking, "This is a sick person who has just turned on me like a rabid animal," you are sitting there feeling the proverbial rug being pulled out from under you. You are thinking, "What did I do? What horrible thing did I do?" You are likely to treat the criticism as though it is real and start trying to fix the problem—if you can. But often you can't. Yes, maybe your feet are on the big side. Yes, sometimes your jokes are lame. Yes, your job is dead-end. And every bit of dismantling makes you feel like a larger and larger pile of useless humanness. What you don't understand is that you are dealing with a narcissistic pattern. One minute the narcissist thinks everything about you is wonderful; the next you are completely flawed.

For some people, this attitude of idealization/de-idealization plays out beyond the primary romantic relationship. JD, for example, says that his wife, Fiona, regularly falls in love with other people, and that even though they have been married for four years, he feels that she has never outgrown what he calls "her adolescent crushes." He says, "Probably the thing that has put the heaviest strain on our relationship is the way Fiona develops these intense relationships with other people. I don't just mean other guys. It also happens with women. Fiona is faithful to me physically, but emotionally—at least eighty percent of the time—she's turned on to somebody else. And she gets very involved with these people. What usually happens is that she meets this new "friend" at some activity, like the gym or the dog park or at work. Then slowly she begins talking about the friend all the time. I'll say something like, 'I had a rough day at work.' She'll say, 'That reminds me of Natasha's day at work,' and she'll be off and running talking about her friend, whoever it might be.

"I can't tell you how many times she has bailed on plans we had because the new friend had some emergency. I'll be home in bed sick, and she'll be running out the door to take care of somebody else. Once, when I had lost my job, she was all excited about this woman, Daphne, who was having money problems because she couldn't pay her credit-card debt. Fiona took money out of our account—which we needed to pay our bills—and she gave it to Daphne. At that point, Fiona talked about Daphne like she was Mother Teresa. It's even worse when it's a guy. Fiona gets crushes on teachers, doctors, and authority figures in general.

"None of this ever lasts very long. Usually within a couple of months, the person does something or says something that Fiona hates. When I ask about the person then, Fiona's attitude is completely different. When she turned off on Daphne, she stopped speaking to her altogether. We usually have a few weeks of peace together, and then there is a new person. It's hard on me. I used to get jealous, particularly of the guys. Now I just don't pay too much attention to it."

Fiona is one of those people who is able to act out her narcissistic need to idealize and then devalue others within the context of a committed relationship, and she is lucky that she has chosen a partner who is relatively tolerant of her pattern. But few narcissists are able to manage this kind of juggling act.

THE NARCISSISTIC QUEST FOR PERFECTION

It's important to understand that everybody has a different idea of what's perfect, and narcissists are no different. One narcissist may be looking primarily for physical beauty or attractiveness;

another may be searching for superior intelligence; still another may want someone with amazing athletic abilities. And, of course, many hope to find impossible combinations—"someone who is incredibly good-looking, intelligent, rich, successful, humble, who loves animals, and shares all my values and preferences." A narcissist with commitment issues will typically think, "I want a commitment with someone who is perfect, or someone who makes me feel perfect."

Narcissists are significantly more aware of the image they project than they are with their own authentic sense of self. They can be incredibly disconnected from any true values or feelings that they might have. This leaves them primarily with surface values. They are so wrapped up in externals that they fail to see others realistically; they frequently have seriously flawed value systems.

When it comes to romance, narcissists are incredibly picky— and usually about the wrong things. They can and will reject wonderful partners for a wide variety of peculiar image issues. Sometimes their fears are based in the here and now. For example, "Sandra has bad taste in clothes, and I'm not sure if I can stay with someone whose sense of style is so different from my own," or "Timothy is only five-foot-eight." I want the father of my children to be tall." Often their fears are based on something that might happen in the future. They are concerned that their partners will not always be the same. Someone like this, for example, may worry excessively that his/her beloved will become fat or bald or get wrinkles. We've known men who have rejected terrific girlfriends because of reasons like, "Suppose she gets fat like her mother?"

Over the years, we've spoken to many people with narcissistic commitment issues about their reasons for ending or wanting to end romantic relationships. Their reasons are almost uniformly based on superficialities. Almost uniformly, they describe the partners who they are rejecting as being good and loving people. Nonetheless, they find something missing, and that something always involves a fantasy of perfection.

CAN SOMEONE LIKE THIS EVER HAVE A WORKABLE RELATIONSHIP?

We've received many questions from people who want to know whether it is ever possible to build a relationship with someone who is commitmentphobic and narcissistic. Our answer is always the same: it depends on *how* commitmentphobic and *how* narcissistic. It's a matter of degree. The worst-case and most toxic commitmentphobic narcissists are rarely able to commit to realistic relationships for any length of time. In those instances where they appear to make commitments, there are usually other factors at play. For example, commitmentphobic narcissists with problems relating to alcohol or substance abuse sometimes stay in one relationship for long periods of time because of dependency issues. Some men and women stay in relationships and handle their conflicts by being incredibly unfaithful; others simply withdraw emotionally.

We also know commitmentphobic narcissists who have drastically changed their patterns as they've grown older. For example, Douglas, a self-admitted commitmentphobic with huge narcissistic issues, had three wives and a couple of live-in girlfriends by the time he was forty. For the next twenty-five years, he broke the hearts of a fair number of other women. At sixty-five, he married a thirty-two-year-old woman, had a child, and claims he is completely reformed. Whether or not Douglas really changed is open to debate.

From our observation, for the most part, commitmentphobics with narcissistic tendencies only change when circumstances force change on them. Some of these people act differently when they meet someone whose behavior is more toxic than their own and become enmeshed in a new, but no less complex and contorted, relationship pattern. Some change if their life circumstances change—financial problems, illness, and aging can all impact on behavior.

So what does this mean for you? It means facing the cold, hard truth about commitmentphobic narcissists. Not every relationship is salvageable. Some partners will only bring us pain. And if you tell yourself that it will be different with you because you are more special or that you are somehow different, then it may very well be your own narcissistic issues doing the talking.

THE DIFFERENCE BETWEEN OLD-FASHIONED COLD FEET AND COMMITMENTPHOBIC NARCISSISM

Isn't everybody at least a little bit scared of long-term commitment? Doesn't everybody start to hyperventilate at the prospect of "till death do us part?" How can you differentiate between an old-fashioned case of cold feet and full-blown commitmentphobia?

In our view, a commitmentphobic narcissist is defined by two things: 1) the intensity by which he/she initially pursues and idealizes a partner, and 2) the intense and traumatic way in which he/she then devalues, turns-off, and/or abandons that same partner.

For example:

• "He called me three times a day to say that he loved me; he told me that I was his reason for being. We were looking at real estate so we could find a place to live in together. Then it was like he dropped off the side of the earth. He didn't return phone calls or e-mails. When I finally tracked him down, he said he didn't know how to tell me that his high school sweetheart had found him online, and they both realized that they had never fully explored their relationship."

• "She was the most loving, giving woman I've ever met, not to mention cute. She said all she wanted was to get married. I had a lot of reservations about moving so fast, but I finally agreed. On Monday, we chose the wedding invitations. On Wednesday, I did something that got her angry—I still haven't figured out what—and she cut me off, cold turkey. No matter how many times I called or how I pleaded, she wouldn't talk to me again. I was like a zombie for months."

If you fall in love with someone who has a fear of commitment combined with narcissistic personality traits, you can expect a bumpy ride at best. What happens when you combine narcissistic idealization with an overriding sense of entitlement and a toxic lack of empathy? You get a lover who at first does everything possible to make you feel as though you have finally found your soul mate, and who then does an 180-degree turn and destroys your hopes and dreams. People like this have a sense of entitlement so huge that they feel justified in whatever they do; people like this have so little empathy that they can't even be sensitive to the pain they have caused. In fact, they are more likely to feel badly for themselves than for you.

Fourteen

IT'S ALL OVER

BREAKUPS ARE HELL, NO MATTER WHAT. RECOVERING from the loss of a love is a tediously exhausting and emotionally debilitating experience. Even when you were the person precipitating the split, you are still dealing with a loss. Even when the person you broke up with was such a major pain that you can't help but feel at least a little bit of relief, you are still dealing with a loss. Sometimes your relationships end even when a breakup is absolutely the last thing in the world that you ever wanted. This can feel so huge that the word *loss* doesn't seem big enough to embrace your state of mind. A bad breakup can be so painful that you feel as though your heart is literally being wrenched out of your chest cavity.

The question is: when you break up with a narcissist, is it a worse split-up than any other? The people we spoke to said that it is, and many of them told us ugly and sad stories about romantic endings. Gina, a forty-two-year-old lawyer who shared some of her experiences, described a romantic breakup that broke and re-broke her heart, and then broke it again. The relationship and the breakup were filled with the kind of drama, conflict, and confusion that go hand in hand with loving a narcissist.

Gina is now happily married to somebody else, and she says she is grateful that she didn't end up with the narcissistic partner she once thought of as the only man for her. Nonetheless, she isn't sure that she will ever fully recover from the trauma of a breakup that took place more than ten years ago. She says, "When I met Jay, I was just twenty-four, and I was already a divorcee and the mother of an adorable four-year-old daughter. My daughter's father and I had gotten married when we were way too young, and it was more than he could handle. My ex-husband wasn't a destructive person, but he was a very reluctant father and husband, and he wanted to go off and be a kid again, which is what he did. So when I met Jay, I was all alone with Holly—that's my daughter's name. I was working two jobs trying to make a living and trying to go to school part-time and trying to be a decent mother. I was totally broke; my ex-husband was giving me a couple of hundred dollars of month for child support, which was all he could afford. I had nobody to help me. I don't have much of a family; my parents were divorced, both had remarried, and neither had either extra time or money. It was extremely tough, and although I wasn't all that upset about not being with my husband, I was really lonely and scared. I also genuinely believed that I had yet to find the man I supposed to be with.

"I met Jay at the library; I was studying for an exam, and so was he. He was almost fourteen years older than me, but he had gone back to school to finish up a graduate degree in business. He had been separated from his ex-wife for such a short time that he didn't even have an apartment yet and was staying with a cousin while he looked for someplace to live. Jay said that his marriage had been miserably unhappy and that his wife put him down constantly. Jay's ex-wife was a doctor, and Jay seemed very proud of that fact. But he said that his wife made him feel inferior because he had trouble finding a career that gave him any real satisfaction, and he didn't make anywhere near as much money as she did during their marriage. He talked about the fact that many of his friends (who he felt were nowhere as smart as he was) were making a lot of money, and while he hated their values, it made him feel like a total failure. I felt very sorry for him, and I tried to do everything I could to build his ego and make him feel good about himself.

"When Jay met me, he acted like he had found the Holy Grail. He couldn't stop talking about how wonderful and beautiful I was, how wonderful my daughter was, and how lucky he was to have met us. He told me he loved me because I was so 'real' and down to earth; he said he needed reality in his life and encouraged us to become an instant little family, and I went along with it. We never really 'dated'; instead, we went from strangers to what felt like intimate partners immediately. It felt 'right' at the time. He was the one who convinced me that we were meant to be together. The things he said and the words he used made me feel that our being together was fated. It was like my prayers were answered.

"At first Jay and I saw each other every Saturday night, and sometimes we would get together for lunch a couple of times a week. Other than that, it was mostly long romantic phone calls. One weekend a month my daughter went with her father so Jay and I had an entire weekend to ourselves. Jay never asked to see me more than that, and since I was so busy and couldn't afford babysitters, I didn't think it was peculiar. In fact, crazy as it seems, I thought he was being sensitive and understanding of my schedule. It didn't even occur to me that he might be dating other women as well as me. When we were together, he was unbelievably romantic and intense and sexual.

"We were going out maybe six months before I really stopped to notice that Jay never ever invited me to go anywhere with him. Sometimes he would inadvertently talk about places he had been and things he had done in the middle of the week. He would mention a concert or a play that he had seen. It began to seem odd that he never suggested that we do anything like that together, even those times that Holly was away for the weekend. I was so incredibly happy to be with him that I didn't need to do anything else, but still, I could tell that he was doing a lot of things with other people but nothing with me. Jay had found an apartment, which I helped him decorate, but we were never there. Most of our time together was at my apartment; for our dates, we would almost always play house. I would make dinner and listen to him talk about whatever he wanted to talk about; he would watch television while I studied; we would read to Holly and put her to bed together.

"When I was invited to anything social, I always took Jay. My friends were people who had children my daughter's age, and most of them were older and closer to Jay's age than mine. Some of them would invite us to parties and other events, and we would spend time with them. One of them owned an incredibly successful real-estate agency, and because he was trying to do something nice for me, he helped Jay get a job in his office. I should mention that Jay was a very good-looking guy and he was a little vain, but he was also very insecure about not having any accomplishments in the business world. After he went into real estate, for the first time in his life Jay began to believe that he could make some serious money, and he started studying for a real-estate license.

"While he was at that office, Jay began to do well financially. That's when he started to change and began acting like he was really hot stuff; he also began spending an enormous amount of money on clothes. The owner's wife was one of my best friends. She reported back to me that she thought that Jay was "playing around" with people he met through work. I never got to verify this because Jay was offered a job for another company, and as soon as he got his license, he changed jobs.

"We were going out for more than a year and a half when Jay's uncle, who I had never met, celebrated his 50th wedding anniversary and made plans for a large party at an expensive hotel. Jay told me about it, but he didn't invite me to go with him. Well, I was devastated. I took it as a total slap in the face. He had become my family. My daughter treated him almost like he was her daddy. We were very good to him. I gave him whatever I had to give. When I told him how upset I was, I was crying so hard I couldn't stop. But he didn't budge. It turns out he had already invited somebody else to go with him—another woman he had met through work. Unlike me, she had money and status and expensive clothes. I threatened to break up with him, and he promised to stop seeing her—*after* his uncle's party. He said that it would be too disruptive to his business relationship with her to break the date.

"That party was the beginning of the end of our relationship, but it took years before it was finally over. After the party, I began to nag Jay about introducing me to his family and incorporating me into his social world, because I was feeling very left out and excluded. I was genuinely shocked that he didn't realize how unhappy he was making me and that he didn't want to do anything to fix it.

"I could no longer pretend not to notice all the things that Jay did that didn't include me. For example, he started to 'court' people that I introduced him to—people he had met through events at my daughter's school and in a way that excluded me. He got himself invited to things and then didn't take me. He seemed to be only interested in people who had a lot of money or some kind of social position. He made me feel like there was something wrong with me. He also made me feel very self-conscious because I didn't have many clothes and those I had weren't expensive. There were no Manolo Blahniks in this New York girl's wardrobe. Once Jay got his real-estate license, he started to clean up financially. He could easily have taken me shopping for clothes if that was all that was bothering him, but he certainly never did anything like that. We began to fight. I wanted more of a commitment, and he didn't want to give it. He said we had met so soon after his divorce, he wasn't really ready. He wanted us to stay just as we were, but he didn't want to promise me anything. Where once he loved me because I was 'real,' now he said that sometimes I presented him with 'too much reality.'

"In the meantime, Jay made plans to take a three week vacation on Nantucket alone, and it put me over the top. I was beginning to feel as though he expected me to be his mother and be happy that he was able to go to nice places—without expecting that he would want to take me, his so-called girlfriend, along. If that's not a mom, what is? We were sitting in a restaurant one night; he was talking to me about a very expensive jacket he had just bought and showing me pictures of the house in which he had taken a share with some other guys. I told him that he was being cruel. He said he was just trying to include me in his plans by showing me what he would be doing. I stood up and walked out of the restaurant without saying a word. When I got home, I didn't answer the phone. I sent him a letter telling him please not to call me again.

"I was deeply hurt and saddened, but I wasn't destroyed. I cried and cried, but I was basically okay. I knew it would take time to heal, but I believed it was a possibility. By then I was working as a paralegal and making more money, and I was getting closer to getting my law degree. I actually had enough money to take Holly away for a week that summer. Of course I also started to think about all the things I might have done wrong in the relationship. I wondered if I had been a little older or more secure financially would things have been different; I wondered if I had made a mistake by not insisting on more of a commitment early in the relationship when Jay was at his most intense.

"After a few months without Jay, I forced myself to go out on a couple of blind dates. Nothing special, but I was able to walk out the door with another man, which felt like a huge accomplishment. I had hope that eventually I would forget Jay and would find somebody else.

"Then I heard through some friends that Jay had met somebody and that he was making plans to marry. That really socked me in the gut, but I was trying to stay strong. Soon after I heard about Jay's new relationship, he started calling me again—often late at night or even in the middle of the night. He said that he was unhappy and wanted to talk to me; he actually said that he needed me to help him move forward with his life. He said that he had met somebody, but he still wanted to work some things out with me. I told him to work them out with his girlfriend. He kept calling. I kept refusing to see him. He told me that he still was in love with me, and that this was 'impeding' his progress. I told him, 'Tough.' Although I was sounding firm when I talked to him, his calls were making me crazy. When I heard his voice I would want to be with him.

"I heard from the same friends that Jay had bought this new woman an engagement ring and that they were looking at condos together. It was hurting me so much. I couldn't help but wonder why he could make a commitment to somebody else that he couldn't make with me. If he loved me, as he said he did, why weren't we together? The next time he called me, it was two A.M. He told me that he and his 'girlfriend' were planning to have children, and he hoped they could have one who was as terrific as Holly, my daughter. I felt like he was kicking me, and he wanted me to just stay there and let him do it. I hung up the phone and from that day forward I screened all my calls. I thought he had lost his mind, and I was completely stressed by our interactions. By that time I had started a flirtation with somebody at work. It was casual and nothing came of it, but at the time, it was helping me hold myself together. Of course I still cried myself to sleep many nights and still wondered if I had done things differently would there have been a different outcome.

"Then two weeks before Christmas, there was a banging at my door at midnight. I looked through the viewer and saw that it was Jay. He was crying. I opened the door, and he grabbed me like he was a drowning man, and he was hanging on for dear life. He couldn't stop crying. He just kept repeating, 'I love you.' It was very melodramatic.

"When he finally stopped crying, we sat up and talked for

most of the night. He told me that he had 'made the biggest mis-take' of his life and that he couldn't stop thinking about me. If I ever had any reconciliation fantasies, and I did, this topped them all.

"We agreed that Jay would immediately go and break up with his 'girlfriend' and that we would start all over. He promised that everything would be different and that this time he wasn't going to mess things up. We had two good weeks; we even spent Christmas together. I was on cloud nine. I felt confident enough to tell everybody that we had reconciled and that everything was going to be okay. I even felt grateful to the woman I now thought was Jay's ex-girlfriend for helping him realize where he was supposed to be.

"A few days before New Year's Eve, Jay told me that he had to tell me something. He said he had to take his ex-girlfriend to a black tie New Year's Eve party because he had promised and it was very important to her. He hoped I would understand. I sort of did understand how tough things must be for her, and if she had this big event why she would need a date—sort of understood it from her point of view. What I didn't understand was why Jay didn't come home to sleep on New Year's Eve, why he wasn't home on the morning of New Year's Day, and why he didn't return my phone calls until late in the evening on New Year's Day. By the time I reached him, I was a wreck. I didn't know if he was somewhere in a ditch or with this other woman. When I finally reached him, he told me that he and the girlfriend needed to give it another try because he hadn't really given it a chance. He said that he couldn't talk to me anymore because I was standing in their way. He acted angry at me, like everything was somehow my fault. After saying that, he said, 'I'm hanging up now.' That sentence and his tone sounded like he didn't want to talk to me . . . ever.

"This time I completely fell apart. I felt as if somebody had cut my heart out of my chest. I was in such pain that I couldn't breathe. I had to talk to him, but he wasn't returning my phone calls. I felt as though he was the only person who could make me feel better. I couldn't work, I couldn't eat, and I couldn't sleep. I lost fifteen pounds in less than a month, and I was thin to begin with. I felt as if I had to do something, so I'm ashamed to say that I got a babysitter and went and stood in front of his apartment house all night waiting for him to come home one night, which he finally did at about seven A.M., just to change for work. I went into his apartment with him, and I'm even more ashamed to say that we made love. It was insane, I was insane; and he was really insane.

"The craziest part was that I blamed myself. I was sure Jay loved me, yet he kept rejecting me. I couldn't help thinking that maybe there was some small thing about me that he just couldn't stand. Maybe if I could fix that, everything would be okay. I also thought that Jay was having a mental breakdown, and that I was somehow at fault. It was like I felt I had to save him from himself, but I didn't know what to do. I used to try to talk about all this with him, but he would just get moody and angry. I got crazy and desperate; I consulted a card reader and an astrologer. I lit candles and I prayed all the time.

"For a few months, we went through this kind of weird period where he was seeing two people and probably telling us both partial truths. She must have been smarter than I was because she eventually broke up with him. With her out of the picture, we more or less resumed our old pattern, but once again he was shutting me out of the rest of his life, and I think he was also dating other people. Then, something big happened. I got pregnant. It was a total accident and birth control failure, because we were both very careful. At first I thought it was like some kind of miracle that would maybe turn him around. I told him that I wouldn't have an abortion; he said that he definitely didn't want a baby. It turns out that I had an ectopic pregnancy and almost died. I was hospitalized for a few days. Fortunately, it was the summer and my daughter was away for a few weeks at her very first sleep-away camp.

"When I got out of the hospital I was still weak and shaky. Jay lived right close to my office, and I asked him if I could please stay at his place for a week so that I wouldn't have to hassle taking subways or buses. He said no. He said something about not feeling comfortable and that we didn't have that kind of relationship. It was very cruel. I knew that Jay was destroying me. I really felt that the failed pregnancy was the result of the stress that I had been under. I used whatever strength I had and once again I refused to take his phone calls; once again I tried to pull myself together, but I was really a basket case from this relationship and this man. Once again, after a short time, he started calling, telling me he missed me and asking to see me.

"I said that I would see him but only if we could see a therapist or counselor together. Jay refused. But by then even Jay realized that he was out of control, and he had gone into therapy for himself with a terrific psychiatrist. I guess Jay must have felt guilty, because although he wouldn't see anybody with me, he suggested that I see his doctor alone without him. He gave his therapist permission to talk to me. I had one session with this doctor, who was very, very skillful and professional, and to whom I will always be grateful. He managed—without giving me any details about Jay's life—to essentially tell me something I should have figured out: that Jay was too narcissistic to have a relationship with anyone. He managed to make me start to see that it wasn't my fault and that there was nothing I had done to make Jay the way he was and nothing I could do to unmake the situation. For some reason I was able to clearly hear and pay attention to what this doctor told me. Maybe I was just ready to hear it. Whatever the reason, this was the beginning of my beginning to let go. Jay and I stopped seeing each other soon after that and although we spoke every now and then, the relationship was over. I got the impression that Jay was already with someone else. For a while I still held out some hope for a miracle, but that was that.

"It took me almost two years before I could even think

about going out with anybody else. I was in mourning and I felt dismembered. Finally I started dating, and I heard through the grapevine that Jay had met somebody else."

One would assume that Gina's relationship with Jay was finally ended and over, but as she tells us, it wasn't. Gina says: "I thought that I would never speak to Jay again, but then I got a big surprise. One morning at work, almost three years since there had been any contact, I picked up the phone, and Jay was on the line. I was stunned. He was back! He started calling me and calling me and calling me. By now I had my law degree and a job so I felt significantly less powerless. Even so, Jay still had the capacity to throw me for a loop. In all of his phone calls he once again said that he had to see me. Once again, I said no. After a few months of his constant phone calling, I agreed to have dinner with him. I remember that I went out and used a charge card to buy an expensive suit just so I would look like one of those women he used to compare me to. How pathetic is that? I expected the dinner to be a disaster, but it wasn't. We had fun, and I could see why I had been so charmed by him in the first place. The morning after that dinner, he called and pleaded with me to give him another chance. He said everything would be different. I just had to trust him. He said all I had to do was be there, and he would do all the work. Once again we started to go out, only this time I wasn't that interested. For about a month, Jay seriously courted me. He was totally attentive. He called every day; he took me places; he took Holly places. I kept going out with him, but I wouldn't go to bed with him.

"Finally, Holly went to spend the weekend with her dad, and Jay came over on a Saturday night. He begged to stay overnight. I said that I still wasn't entirely sure. I told him that I was worried that the minute I went to bed with him, he would go back to his old routine. He cried and said that would never happen. 'Do you have any idea how much I love you?' he said. He took my face between both his hands and looked straight into my eyes. 'Do you really think I would do that?' Tears were streaming down his face. Finally I agreed. He spent the night, and we spent the next day together. He left at about six o'clock Sunday evening. He didn't call Monday or the next day or the next. By now, I wasn't even surprised. I think I was actually relieved. Even so, two weeks later I called him. 'I think I deserve some kind of an explanation,' I told him. He said, 'I decided that it was never going to work out between the two of us.' I asked him, 'When were you planning to tell me?' 'Well I'm telling you now.'

"It was finally finished. The end. I still feel very guilty that I allowed him to enter my life. For years I was a mental wreck, which had to affect my daughter. Now I know, really know, that he was just terrible to me. I was a young woman with a sweet vulnerable child, and we both loved him. I never did anything to hurt him. He did nothing for me: he lied, he cheated, he used, and he abused my love. He kept promising me his love and then he kept taking it away, and he did it again and again. I know that I was stupid, but he was really disgusting. I still hear from him every now and then. He calls me whenever he wants free legal advice. Now, when I hear his voice, I try to figure out why I was so much in love with him. I must have been nuts."

Many men and women who have ended relationships with narcissistic partners can identify with the drama as well as the ups and downs that Gina describes. They can also identify with the confusion she describes as she tried to understand what was going on with a partner who talked about love and higher values, but whose behavior reflected selfishness and self-interest.

WHY BREAKING UP WITH A NARCISSIST IS ESPECIALLY DIFFICULT

We asked people why they thought breaking up with a narcissist was particularly painful. Here are some of the reasons they gave:

• You never really understand what happened or why it didn't work; you lack a sense of closure.

Relationships with narcissists tend to be more about promise and potential than they are about the kind of real stuff that happens between two people who are trying to forge a working connection. Men and women who have been in love with narcissists often say that they feel as though their relationships never played through; they say that they don't believe that the relationship had run its course. Instead, it almost feels as though the relationship was just getting started and needed only the slightest push to get off the ground and soar. That push never seemed to happen. A common statement we have heard is, "We *could have had* such a great relationship if only . . ."

In many troubled relationships, both partners know exactly what is wrong. In these relationships, there are concrete ways in which the couple disagree, whether it be about money, religion, sex, politics, where to live, or how to live. Relationships with narcissists rarely reach the kind of plateau where a couple is arguing about anything real. When people argue with their narcissistic partners, they are usually complaining about behavior that is primarily reflecting the narcissist's unwillingness to be in a real relationship.

Splitting up with a narcissist is particularly difficult because the relationship you were promised never happened, and you don't know why. Since you never feel as though you shared a real relationship, how can you understand what did or didn't take place? Trying to get explanations from narcissists can be an incredibly frustrating endeavor. Even in their breakups, narcissists tend to be unwilling to give any sense of closure. They are typically unwilling or unable to explain what happened because they don't understand it, either. They also don't understand your discomfort in not having any real answers, nor do they want to.

• **You don't understand why your partner refuses to do anything to save the relationship.**

You know that there is a lot of good stuff between you and your partner. So why won't your partner go with you to a therapist or counselor? Why won't your partner work with you to resolve your difficulties?

You may hope that if you could get your partner into a therapist's office, there would be a positive outcome. You might think that if somebody other than you explained the situation, your partner would have an "aha" moment of clarity and understanding. Under these circumstances, perhaps you and your partner would be able to communicate and find ways to smooth out your problems. But, for the most part, nothing you say and nothing you do seems to get your partner into a therapist's office; or, if your partner does agree to making an appointment, chances are that he/she will go for one or two sessions and then find something wrong with the process or the therapist. In a few rare instances, the narcissist will consult a therapist, but will somehow manage to sabotage the entire process.

Narcissists typically don't think they have a problem. That's why they don't want to visit counselors or therapists. They don't want to work to fix their relationships because they don't want things to be any different. They want to stay in that space that allows them to live in fantasyland and swing from idealization to de-idealization. Many narcissists always have at least one foot out the door of any relationship they are in, and they don't want anyone to call them on their behavior. They don't want to be held accountable. They don't want reality or a realistic process such as therapy or counseling to interfere with their way of operating. This is usually more important to them than any relationship.

• **You can't figure out why your partner seems angry at you.**

She's the one who cheated. He's the one who lied. She's the one who left you sitting at the airport for six hours. He's the one who borrowed money to buy a new car and then wouldn't return either the car or the money. Why are these totally selfish, self-involved people angry at you?

yeah

* Most likely you have touched a nerve that your partner didn't want touched. When you get too close to a narcissist, you run the risk of touching the rage they feel coming from their essential narcissistic injury. It's also a good idea to remember that narcissists don't take responsibility. They always have a way of justifying their behavior and blaming the other person. If your partner was unfaithful for example, he/she may blame you for not stopping them or for not having been available on the night that they met the new person. A narcissist is fully capable of thinking or saying something like, "Is it my fault you were home taking care of the new baby on the night I went to that party? I was feeling alone and neglected."

Many narcissists have also figured out that their anger is a way of manipulating the other person. They know that if they appear to have any justification on their side, there is a chance that others will back down. The worst-case narcissists are consciously manipulative—and, from their point of view, this all-about-me approach to life is justifiable.

• **It feels as though nothing that happened between the two of you was real.** *True!*

Your partner presented himself or herself as one kind of person, but now your partner isn't acting like that person. Was that presentation real? Your partner told you that he/she cared about you and your feelings. But now your partner doesn't seem to care at all. Were any of your partner's words real? Was the passion real? Was the intensity real? How about the feeling that you were soul mates conjoined for eternity? Was that real? WAS ANY OF IT REAL? *I'm almost at the place of surely saying no*

You probably see your partner's initial presentation of himself or herself as being true and real. You want to find ways to encourage your partner to be that person. In fact, you may well think that if you can bring your partner back to that place, you will be bringing him or her back to reality. Let's start by telling you that your partner's initial presentation cannot be counted on to be real. It was a sales presentation, no more and no less. As for your partner's feelings, remember that narcissists have a highly evolved sense of drama, but very shallow feelings. All that passion, all that intensity, all those words were more about drama than they were about feelings. So, yes, there was probably an abundance of unreality involved in all the drama. As for your soul-mate dreams, we don't want to be harsh, but chances are that these were fanned a least a little bit by your own Hollywood scenarios and fantasies.

The thing you need to remember is that narcissists are not interested in reality. They may be attracted to it; they may be fascinated by it; and they may pay lip service to its value. But they run from it, creating what can almost appear as studies in perpetual motion. Many narcissists act as though their very survival is dependent on their continuing to live in a place that is separate from reality. That's a place where the only image they are really interested in is their own.

- **Your partner acts as though he/she wants you to continue to be loving and supportive even as you are being rejected.**

In a reasonable adult relationship, everything flows two ways—back and forth between the two partners. In a relationship with a narcissist, everything flows one way—toward the narcissist. Narcissists expect you to behave this way no matter what they do.

This is incredibly confusing to the rejected partner. It feels like a double message. It feels as though you are being invited to stay intimate, despite the split up. You may believe that your partner is having some kind of breakdown and continues to need you. You are likely to think, "Oh, my partner still needs me. He/she is letting me know that he/she wants to maintain the connection. My partner still wants my love, no matter what he/she is doing."

In all likelihood you have been totally accepting and

supportive in your relationship, and your narcissistic partner wants you to continue to be that way. Why not?

But it isn't good for you, and it's highly improbable that it's going to get you what you need. This is a time to protect and take care of yourself. Let go of the burden of being the person who is expected to be all-supportive and all-loving. Just let it go. I agree

Yes, your partner may seem reluctant to let you go even as you are being pushed away. Yes, your narcissistic partner may well be unwilling to completely cut you lose. It's true that he/she doesn't want you to disappear totally. This is because you fulfill a function. This is about manipulation, not partnership.

- **You can't get over the feeling that you did something wrong or that you are somehow responsible for not making the relationship work.**

Narcissists frequently conduct their relationships as though they are conducting prolonged job interviews. By definition, narcissists are critical and contemptuous of others. It's not unusual for them to be particularly critical of the people who love them. What this means is that if you are in love with a narcissist, you may never feel as though you are getting the "grade" you deserve. Chances are that your narcissistic partner always finds ways to make you feel as though you failed. This may be very obvious, or it may have been done very subtly. The end result, however, is that you become accustomed to the feeling that you have to keep proving yourself.

Once the relationship is over, you may still be second-guessing everything you do. You may be thinking, "If only I had done this—or that." Be assured that no matter what you did or didn't do, your narcissistic partner would have started dismantling you. Your relationship didn't end because of anything that happened. It ended because of who and what your partner is.

- **Your partner has no respect for what you shared together.**

Martha has just told George that she is leaving him after ten years of marriage. During those years, George has supported everything Martha wanted. He even worked two jobs so she could become a dentist. Now Martha says that she needs a new and better model husband.

"But," George says, "how can you be so cruel? Don't you remember everything I did so that you could see your dreams fulfilled?"

Martha replies, "I would have found a way to go to dental school even without you. So I don't think you should take any credit. And how dare you put me down by implying that you had anything to do with my success. I did this with my hard work, not yours. All you gave was money, and if you hadn't, I would have figured out another way."

In short, it doesn't matter what you do, what you shared, or what deals you made; your narcissistic partner sees the world from a totally self-referential, it's all-about-me point of view. As far as your partner is concerned, if you have reached a place where you are no longer fulfilling a function, your partner is capable of obliterating you and your history together. He/she can't hear a word you are saying. It's almost like you don't exist. That's just the way it is. Remember the myth of Narcissus and Echo. Think about how Narcissus completely tuned Echo out. As far as he was concerned, she wasn't even there. Narcissists can wipe out you and the history of your relationship in exactly the same way. We know that this feels hurtful, but it's just the way narcissists behave.

- **You feel as though your partner doesn't see you realistically and doesn't know who you are.**

We talked to a woman named Laura whose narcissistic boyfriend recently rejected her, saying she wasn't "artistic" enough for him. Laura has a degree in art history and is a talented painter who had given up painting full-time because she needs to make a living. Laura doesn't know what her boyfriend is talking about. All she knows is that in the artistic department, she feels as though she could be whatever he wanted her to be.

She feels as though she needs to prove her artistic worth to her ex-boyfriend. She feels that if she could get him to see her realistically, for the person she is, he would love and accept her.

When you met your narcissistic partner, you probably felt as though you had a soulmate connection. You felt as though he/she could see and appreciate you for who and what you are. This is part of the narcissistic connection. But when narcissists end their relationships, they often find something wrong with their partners. This "something" is almost inevitably something that seems stupid and unreal. An artist is rejected for not being artistic, so she says, "Watch me, I can be as artistic as you want." A brunette is rejected for not being blonde, so she buys a bottle of hair dye and says, "I can become a blonde." A good-natured man with a great sense of humor is rejected because he "isn't serious enough. "I can be serious," he says. "I'm as serious as the next person, but I cover it up. Give me a chance." A decorated war hero is rejected because he isn't aggressive enough.

When narcissists reject their partners in this way, they take back that sense of being seen and accepted that existed at the beginning of the relationship. If you are the person who is being rejected suddenly instead of feeling totally "known" and "seen," you feel as though you're completely misunderstood; you feel as though you are not being "seen" for who you are. You may even feel as though you are rendered invisible and powerless.

Men and women who are rejected in this way typically respond by trying to prove themselves. They try to get their partners to look at them realistically. But it's not going to happen. This is an exercise in futility that can only make you feel worse. The most painful part, of course, is that sense of being seen and understood at the beginning of the relationship is destroyed.

• **Any tendencies you have to be jealous are being fanned by your partner's behavior.**

Jealousy is one of the most awful emotions any of us can ever experience. We could give you lots of advice about trying to relax and let go of your jealousy, but we know how big a challenge this is—particularly if you have just split up with a narcissist. Toxic narcissists seem to have an especially difficult time being alone. As soon as they end one relationship, they are likely to quickly catapult themselves into another.

Also remember that narcissists love attention, and what better way to grab attention than to have two people fighting over you. What this means is that not only is the narcissist in your life likely immediately to get involved with another person—or several other people, for that matter, but he/she will probably manage to bring it to your attention in some particularly brutal and hurtful way. In fact, narcissists sometimes engage in a series of games that make their ex-partners acutely aware of everything they are doing.

The other reason why jealousy plays such a major part in any breakup with a narcissist is your worry that somebody else will reap the rewards. You fear that someone else will get the relationship you were promised; you are concerned that your ex-partner will miraculously have been turned into a loving and giving human being who is capable of being part of a relationship that you would want. This thought may have the power to gnaw away at your insides. This kind of thinking is one of the most self-destructive things you can do to yourself. We can't assure you that narcissists never get involved in other relationships, but we can assure you that the likelihood of a narcissist getting involved in the kind of relationship that would make you happy is almost nonexistent. Fight the jealousy and work at building a good life for yourself.

• **You feel as though he/she is the only person who can make you feel better.**

The end of your relationship may have left you feeling powerless as well as heartbroken. But the strangest thing you feel is a sense that only the person who has made you feel so terrible can make you feel whole again. That's because, for a brief moment, you thought you had a soulmate connection with someone who saw and connected to the inner you. No matter what your partner does or says, you may believe that this connection still exists. You want this connection returned to you, and the only person who can do it is your rejecting partner.

It's almost impossible to believe your partner doesn't feel everything you feel. It doesn't seem conceivable that your partner was simply acting out narcissistic impulses when you were so deeply touched. We've heard people describe this connection and the feelings it engenders as being almost otherworldly. The problem is that no matter how strongly you may be reverberating from this connection, your partner seems able to turn it off and on at will.

A large part of your healing process revolves around your coming to realize that while a narcissistic partner can make you feel sick, he/she is not capable of helping you do any real healing. That's just the way it is.

HEALING TAKES TIME

We promise you that you will heal; we promise you that you will reach the point where you will wonder how you could have possibly found this person attractive, interesting, or desirable. We promise you that you will eventually be grateful that you didn't have to spend your life with this self-absorbed and selfish person. We cannot promise you that this will happen overnight, but we know that it will happen.

For yourself, focus on the healing process. Be good to yourself and take care of your own mental health. Don't pick at scabs; try to stop examining and re-examining the relationship. Find people to support you through this process; do things that feel positive and constructive; and stay realistic and grounded.

One final bit of advice: don't blame yourself for your ex-partner's behavior. The insight that is going to make all of this easier for you revolves around your awareness and understanding of narcissism. Nothing you did or said created this narcissism; nothing you can be, do, or say will make it disappear.

Fifteen

DON'T LET IT HAPPEN AGAIN!

HAVE YOU RECENTLY ENDED A RELATIONSHIP WITH a narcissist, or are you in the process of ending one? If either is the case, you probably realize by now that you may be particularly vulnerable. We personally think that if you are observant and stay grounded in reality at the beginning of a relationship, you will be able to spot many clues to warn you about the potential for narcissistic behavior down the road. This is good information for those of you who are thinking of dating again; it can also help those of you who have recently started dating someone about whom you have some serious reservations.

We've talked to a lot of men and women about their relationships with toxic narcissists. Most of them say that when they first started going out with these people, they definitely noticed behavior that they chose to ignore. The primary reason they didn't pay attention? They were too busy being swept off their feet.

Julia wants all our female readers to know that she has, on at least one occasion, walked into a bad relationship while ignoring scads of information that should have put her on guard.

She says, "Let me tell you all about a blind date I once

had that progressed to a disastrous relationship. I consider this one totally my fault because I should never have let it continue beyond the first thirty minutes.

"We all make mistakes, and I like to believe that what's important is that we learn from them and move on. With that in mind, I once made the mistake of getting involved with a deceptive guy whose sense of entitlement could have swallowed Kansas. He simply never felt that he had to be accountable for anything he said or did, and I had all the information I needed on the first date.

"For our first date, Keith and I were supposed to meet at the bar of an elegant restaurant on the upper east side of Manhattan. I got there five minutes late, feeling totally guilty. This was a blind date, so I didn't have any idea what Keith would look like. I saw a man sitting at the bar and walked up to him. Wrong guy. I sat down, ordered a glass of wine, pulled out a magazine, and started sipping. After about twenty-five minutes of this, I was happily ready to give up. I started to pay for the wine and was about to leave when my blind date hurried in.

"'I'm sorry,' he said, 'but I got stuck in traffic.' Okay, I thought. This can happen to anybody. In the back of my head I remembered that we had chosen the place to meet based on what he told me about living within a five minute walking distance, but I thought that he might have been coming from someplace else. And it would certainly have been totally 'not cool' of me to grill him to get an explanation. Some of you may notice that we had only known each other five minutes, and I was already making excuses for him.

"We sat down and began to chat about world events, the person who had introduced us, and several other people who it turned out we both knew. After ten minutes of this kind of chitchat, a good-looking woman walked past us on her way out of the restaurant area. She stopped when she reached the bar. 'Keith,' she said. Keith turned. He seemed totally uncomfortable. 'Renee,' he said. He introduced us. Renee, who looked as though she was about to cry, nodded nervously in my direction. 'I've been calling you for four weeks straight,' she said, 'and you haven't returned one call.'

"Keith started to mumble something about having been busy. This was turning into an awkward scene at best. From Renee's and Keith's body language, I could see that she felt that he had hurt her deeply. I could also see that he was annoyed and embarrassed by her popping up the way she did.

"I excused myself and said that it looked like they had stuff to talk about.

"Keith looked uncertain and finally said, 'I'll call you.'

"I left the bar thinking that he was definitely a bad-news guy who should be avoided. Nonetheless, when he left a message on my machine the following morning, I returned the call. I told myself that it would be impolite not to do so. Keith apologized profusely, telling me that Renee was indeed an ex-girlfriend. After going out with her, he said he realized that he had to avoid 'needy' women. He told me that Renee was a good woman, but that she wanted more than he wanted to give—at least not to her. He said that he had probably handled the breakup badly, and he was sorry about that. But he didn't know what he was supposed to do. She wouldn't have accepted anything he told her anyway. He told me that he really needed a woman who could stand on her own two feet—somebody more like me. He also indicated that he wasn't like some other guys he knew who weren't really sensitive to women. He told me that he liked women and tried very hard to understand what the women in his life were feeling. At that moment it did cross my mind that he wasn't very 'sensitive' to Renee when he refused to take her phone calls. I thought it, but I didn't say it.

"At that point I should have said, 'STOP, RIGHT THERE!' and hung up. But I didn't. He was so charming, smart, and seductive that I stayed on the phone. He flattered me, and he flattered my ego. Nobody likes hanging up on somebody who flatters their ego. That's how I plunged forward into one short-lived and totally stupid relationship."

RED FLAGS

Do you think that you can become so adept at spotting narcissism that you will be able to notice the signs within the first few dates? Obviously it's difficult to come to any completely reliable conclusions about anybody on such a basis. Nonetheless, people with narcissistic issues typically wave one of several clear-cut red flags that you would be wise to notice. Many of these can be observed on the very first date, but it is possible that they won't show up until date three.

If you meet somebody who you think is showing signs of narcissism, it doesn't mean that you have to walk away immediately. Just don't throw caution to the wind. Get more information to make sure. When it comes to giving your heart away, we have always advised our readers not to be so quick to jump into the deep water. Wade in slowly, take your time, and pay attention to what's going on. We've said this before, but we'll say it again: if you think you are being offered the relationship of a lifetime, you'll have a lifetime to enjoy it, so take it slow. Yes, it's important to stay open to finding love, but that doesn't mean giving your heart away to a stranger. No precious parts need be given away until you learn more. There is a difference between falling in love with love and falling in love with a real flesh-and-blood human being. You have to keep both your mind and your heart open to reality as well as the promise of love. Always pay attention to *everything* that you are feeling and noticing. And, until you know for sure, don't override that little voice that points out warning signs.

SOME NARCISSISTIC WARNING SIGNALS THAT CAN BE OBSERVED EARLY IN THE RELATIONSHIP

- **Does your potential partner do or say anything that indicates that he/she wants to control the relationship and expects** everything you do to be organized around his/her wishes and schedule?

This quality can be expressed in very subtle ways that often seem perfectly reasonable. For example, you may think, "It's perfectly reasonable for James to ask me to meet him at his house instead of mine as originally planned. After all, he's been working all day." Or, "It's perfectly reasonable for Jill to change plans and expect me to spend the evening at her mother's house watching her cousin's home video. All that really matters is that we are together." This logic is certainly valid, but if James (or Jill) always has an agenda that is given preferential treatment, you may very well be dealing with a narcissist.

In an ideal relationship, when it comes to making plans, both partners hear and acknowledge what is important to each other. They nurture and support each other; they find ways to cooperate and compromise. Since we don't live in a perfect world, and nobody has a 100 percent equal partnership, most of us have to be satisfied with a little less than the ideal. However, narcissists find it incredibly difficult to truly hear their partners. This means that narcissists almost always have agendas that ignore what their partners want while setting up relationships that are organized around their wishes, schedules, and peculiarities. The more toxic the narcissist, the more glaring and observable this quality.

Try to pay attention during your first few dates. That's when your partner is likely to be on his/her best behavior. Don't forget that self-centered behavior tends to escalate not diminish. Does your potential partner do any of the following?

- Manipulate all scheduling to fit his/her wishes.
- Change plans and times repeatedly to fit his/ her wishes or scheduling.
- Find excuses to keep from doing whatever you would like to do while expecting you to go along with whatever he/she wants.
- Insist on restaurants that you can't afford and then expect you to pay for half or all of the bill.

- Engage in any inappropriate attention-getting behavior, including drinking too much.
- Conveniently run out of money, expect you to pay, and then forget to pay you back.
- Ignore your appropriate and reasonable sleep and work schedule and insist on your accompanying him/her to events or activities that will create havoc in your life.
- Use his/her lateness as a way of reorganizing your life and priorities.
- Make his/her work, sleep, health, or neurosis the organizing issue in the relationship.

• Does your potential partner have a presentation about his/her life that seems almost rehearsed?

We repeat: narcissists often have stories about their lives that are gripping, engrossing, and involving. They have a way of telling these stories to perfect strangers who they are interested in knowing better. Each time they tell their well-practiced stories, it's as if they are telling them for the first time—instead of the hundredth. They know when they are being charming; they know when they are being convincing; and they know when they appear to be showing "emotional depth." They can make events that happened years and years ago appear immediate and compelling. Some narcissists' eyes even manage to well up at exactly the same place after years of telling the same story.

Yes, we all like to talk about ourselves at least a little bit. Yes, when we find someone with whom we feel a connection, we want to open up and share our souls. Yes, there is nothing wrong—and everything right—with letting people we love know who we are.

So how do you know when you're getting a narcissistic presentation as opposed to an honest sharing?

Well, unless you're genuinely psychic, you really can't know for sure, but there are certain things that should make you more cautious and careful about giving your heart until you have more information. For example, if total strangers start telling you what appear to be their deepest secrets within the first thirty minutes, be appropriately wary. People who are sincere often have a difficult time opening up that quickly, no matter who is sitting across the table.

Many narcissists organize their relationships around their "problems." If total strangers press you for advice on their current problems within thirty seconds and behave as though you are the only one who understands, be more than a bit wary. Remember narcissists have a way of using their "stories," problems, and issues to grab center stage. Even though this attractive new person is talking to you with high intensity and making you feel as though he/she has never been able to talk this way to anyone else ever, be careful. People who are able to weave a gripping and self-serving tale about their lives and their problems often have had a great deal of practice.

• **Does your potential partner manage to let you know all the ways in which he/she is special?**

Narcissists tend to make sure that you know everything about them that could be deemed "great" or unique. They will tell you how others consider them good-looking, extremely smart, extraordinarily compassionate, unbelievably bold and courageous, talented, incredibly rich and successful, etc. It's all presentation. Narcissists tend to define and position themselves the way they want to be seen. Some have no qualms about stretching reality a bit. When Brian first met Grace, for example, he impressed on her that he was a good guy and made a point of telling her that he regularly visited his next door neighbor, an invalid, to help out with shopping and errands. Grace took Bob at his word. A couple of months later when she was visiting him, she met the next door neighbor's wife, and discovered just how much Bob helped out. The truth was that on two occasions over a three-year period, when Bob went to the store to get the Sunday papers, he picked up the neighbor's paper as well.

If you get involved with a narcissist, you will probably not immediately notice that you aren't given much of an opportunity to find things out about them on your own. They are more likely to tell you what "good" people they are rather than "show" you with their actions. Relationships with narcissists aren't about growth and genuine exploration of mutual interests.

• **Is your potential partner given to idealization and romantic fantasies?**

This is an incredibly important characteristic to notice. As we've said before, romantic fantasies tend to revolve around a "love scenario" that happens too quickly. Romantic fantasies tend to feature almost immediate inclusiveness and excessive use of the "we" word, for example, as in, "We will go here; we will do that." If you are involved with someone who is given to idealization and romantic fantasies, you may well be swept away by his/her ardor and seduction.

If you are the person who is being idealized, it's difficult to stand back and believe this is a negative thing. However, if your potential partner is all about fantasy with no realistic base, you have a potential problem. We all want to believe in romance and soul mates, but don't let your need to believe in these things overcome your common sense. Remember that narcissists often follow up idealization with de-idealization and dismantling. So give your relationship time to deepen and grow; give yourself a chance to make sure that your new partner sincerely wants to build a sound relationship based on reality and love.

• **Does your potential partner have values that seem to be superficial or based primarily on how things appear?**

Is your potential partner overly focused on how you or others look? Does he/she place too much value on clothing, makeup, hair styles, etc.? Is your potential partner too concerned with his/her own appearance?

Narcissists tend to have shallow emotions and values. This can be difficult to spot because narcissists often say one thing and do another. It's not uncommon, for example, for someone with serious narcissistic issues to put down others for caring too much about makeup, clothing, furnishings, and status while at the same time stressing those very same things in his/her own life. So pay attention. Is it possible that there is a huge discrepancy between what your potential partner *says* and what he/she *does*?

Many men and women with narcissistic issues sometimes show their superficiality by attaching labels to people, much as one would to clothing. You can spot this if your potential partner tends to name-drop or attach a label-like description to everybody he/she talks about. For example, "Let me tell you about my friend Fredric, who is the richest person in Santa Monica." Or "Last night my friend Doreen, who is one of the most gorgeous women in this city, threw a party for her friends—Stephanie, who is a swimsuit model, and Sammy, who is a published author who has been on Dr. Phil."

- **Is your potential partner too good a salesperson?**

Selling is selling, and there is a reason why good salespeople make the big bucks.

Here is a question to ask yourself about the first time you and your potential partner sit down to talk: does it feel like a conversation or a sales pitch? Ask yourself if this potential partner is behaving like someone who wants to close a sale. Is he/she going too far in trying to impress you? Is he or she trying too hard to convince you to buy the goods that are being sold?

You may pride yourself on being smart and well-defended. This quality may make you more interesting to narcissists while they are in their idealization phase; it may make them work even harder to break down your defense system.

• **Does your potential partner make you feel as though he/she has immediately formed a different and "special" relationship with you?**

We've said this before, but we'll say it again for emphasis. The most telling feature in a narcissist's repertoire is the ability to convey a sense of "specialness." When narcissists are in their idealization mode, they tend to make you feel both cherished and admired. They make you feel as though you are understood and appreciated. For example, often narcissists will immediately let you know that they have been less than perfect with previous partners, but their words and actions reassure you that it will be different with you.

Maybe you and your new partner are "fated" to be together, but if this is the case, nothing is going to happen if you stay cautious and self-protective.

• **Does your potential partner do anything that seems to be "testing" in terms of how much he/she can get away with?**

"Testing" behaviors can show up pretty early. Here are some of the most common:

- Drinking too much.
- Talking too much.
- Obviously spending more than he/she can afford.
- Not having enough money to pay his/her share of the check, which leaves you paying the bill.
- Flirting with other people, including the waitperson.
- Asking you to do the kind of favor one normally reserves for old friends and family.
- Any inappropriate, attention-getting behavior.
- Careless and/or dangerous driving.

How about what your potential partner tells you about his/her past? Are you told about how "testing" behavior, such as chronic infidelity, destroyed previous relationships?

• **Does your potential partner seem genuinely interested in hearing about you?**

Does your potential partner encourage you to talk about yourself, or are you always being shut down? Some narcissists are so self-involved that they never, ever, seem to want to know anything about anyone else. Others are not so obvious. Dave, for example, says that Brianna always asks him questions about himself, but when he starts to answer, she interrupts or changes the subject. If you have met somebody who does too much of the talking, and who tells you how interested he/she is in you but yet seems to have no interest in anything you might say, it's a pretty safe bet that there are some narcissistic issues at play.

And if you meet somebody who is completely self-referential, as in "my job," "my house," "my cat," "my dog," "my problems," and "my interests," don't expect this person ever to show any real interest in you or your life. Remember this, even if the person is incredibly cute and charming.

• **Does your potential partner show any signs of inappropriate boundaries?**

It is a given that people with strong narcissistic issues have boundary issues, and this often shows itself early on. The first time they visit your home, they may immediately take over and act as if it is their own. They may almost assume possession of your property in a way that seems extremely intimate. When Felice went out on her first date with Toby, for example, they made plans for her to pick him up in her car. When she arrived, he said, "I'd rather drive, if you don't mind." At first she thought, *Gee, I don't even know this guy,* but instead of being annoyed, Felice was flattered. She thought Toby was a take-charge man who wasn't afraid of intimacy. She thought his behavior indicated that he would be someone with whom she could share things. When Felice knew Toby only a few days, he seemed to want to be included in everything she did; she was surprised, for example, that he wanted to go with her to a doctor's appointment. It goes without saying that three months later, she could not get him to go with her to a movie.

A narcissist's issues with boundaries can show up early on with money. He/she might inappropriately expect you to pay for too many things. Wes, for example, went out on a blind date with a woman, and he paid for dinner. Before they left the restaurant, she ordered two takeout dinners and several desserts to take home for her mother and sister, and she expected Wes to pay for everything.

The most obvious boundaries in romantic relationships revolve around sex. Narcissists are often inappropriately sexual very early in the relationship. This can seem intimidating and a little bit scary, but it is also flattering; it can seem as though he/she is overcome by your charms. In reality, it's most likely to be an example of bad boundaries. Think about how arrogant somebody has to be in order to be so overtly and fearlessly sexual with someone he/she barely knows. Think about how experienced he/she must be.

Some narcissists quickly exhibit a point of view that can best be described as, "What's mine is mine, and what's yours is also mine." They may take over your life, your car, your house, and your money, but draw deep lines in the sand when it comes their lives and their belongings.

Some narcissists can behave in exactly the opposite manner. They may invite you into their lives, but refuse to have anything to do with yours. Without any valid reasons, they act as if everything about your life, from your family to your friends to your living space, is inferior or lacking. Everything has to be done on their turf.

• **Does your potential partner exhibit any obvious attention getting behavior?**

Somebody doesn't have to get drunk, put a lampshade on his head, and dance around the room to get attention. There are so many equally effective techniques that narcissists use to get attention. Lateness, which serves many purposes, is a favorite. Flamboyant behavior, excessive spending, name dropping, grandiose stories, inappropriate flirting are some others. One of the narcissistic classics is to create chaos in order to get attention.

Attention-getting behavior is usually disruptive and frequently manipulative. For example, Ben says that his ex-wife, Sada, had a wide variety of almost imaginary ailments that she would trot out whenever she wanted attention or wanted to get her own way. He said that on their first date, she developed a headache when he suggested a restaurant she didn't like. It miraculously disappeared when they decided on one she did like. He said that was definitely a clue, which he unfortunately chose to ignore.

- **Does your potential partner have an extreme, over-the-top sense of entitlement?**

Narcissists sometimes reveal their sense of entitlement by the way they treat other people. Does your potential partner, for example, cut through lines to get in front of people or insist that a waitperson take care of your table first? Narcissists want to receive preferential treatment, and if they don't, they can become extremely annoyed or downright angry. In many ways, full-blown narcissists are like temperamental children who suffer from low frustration tolerance. They expect everything to go *their* way. A traffic jam or other drivers, for example, can disrupt their moods. How could there be traffic? How could that other driver cut in like that? Don't they understand whose agenda they are disrupting?

Many narcissists show their sense of entitlement by flaunting rules and regulations. They don't feel that they have to do what other people do. Many feel that they are so special that they don't have to meet any kind of minimal expectation, from showing up on time to showing up sober. They like to think that rules are for other people. When Gary, for example, wanted to get a job as a social worker in a Spanish-speaking community, he was outraged that one of the things required of applicants was that they be bilingual: "Why should I have to learn another language? Shouldn't *they* be the ones to learn how to communicate with me?

In general, society's rules and expectations can be distressing to narcissists. A narcissist with drinking issues might say, "I can drink as much as I want. I don't have to listen to anybody else." That same person might later go on to say, "I can drink and drive. I don't need to stay off the road." Someone with spending issues would say, "I can buy what I want when I want."

The bottom line is that narcissists think that everything that they feel, everything that they want, and everything that they need is more important for them than for anybody else. That's entitlement.

• Does your potential partner show signs of being overly jealous or envious or contemptuous of others?

Remember that narcissists tend to both idealize and devalue others, so look for extremes. Just because your potential partner is all positive and glowing about somebody doesn't mean that he/she will not later switch to a more negative point of view. Listen closely: when this person talks about others, does he/she seem unusually contemptuous? Are there words and phrases used that one associates with criticism? Does this person have the capacity to be hurtfully sarcastic? Just because it's not directed at you for the moment doesn't mean that it won't be in the future.

How about jealousy and envy? Does your potential partner seem to be too invested in tearing down other people's accomplishments? Does he/she seem both jealous and disdainful of other people's success? When something nice happens to somebody else, is he/she capable of being happy for another person?

• **Does your potential partner do something that is downright inconsiderate and disruptive of your plans—even with a good excuse?**

Allison says that Kevin told her he loved her on their second date. The next day, a Saturday, was her son's fifth birthday. When Kevin asked if he could see her, Allison told him about the small birthday party her mother was giving for her son. Allison asked Kevin if he wanted to come with them. Kevin said, "Yes." It was agreed that he would come to her house and pick Allison and her son up to take them to the party. When he was fifteen minutes late, Kevin called from his cell phone and said he was on his way. When he was thirty minutes late, Kevin called and said he would be there right away. When he was an hour late, Kevin called and said he was at Kmart trying to buy a present for the little boy. After an hour and thirty minutes, after Kevin phoned again to say he was stuck in traffic, Allison called a car service.

IT'S A TOUGH WORLD OUT THERE!

If you have ever been in love with a narcissist, you probably already know that at least part of what propelled you forward into a troubled relationship were your own good intentions and lack of cynicism. You also know how your soul-mate fantasies worked against your emotional well-being. You want to believe in the possibility of love, and you want to believe in the inherent goodness of the people you meet. You want to give the other person "a chance." Yet, scores of well-intentioned and loving men and women like you have given up years of their lives "taking care" of narcissistic demands and agendas. Keep this in mind when you are in the process of dating and meeting new people. Of course you want love, but you want a love that is true and real and two-sided.

Yes, it's wonderful that you are so eager to love and be loved, but don't let that keep you from being reasonably self-protective, particularly when you meet someone who is unusually attentive or who uses words to cast a spell that evokes the promise of love.

Sixteen

ARE YOU STAYING OR LEAVING?

S OMETIMES MEN AND WOMEN PICK UP A BOOK like this one because they are trying to make tough decisions about which direction they should take. Should they hunker down with their narcissistic partners and try even harder to make the relationship work? Or should they pack up their bags, pick up their marbles, and move on?

If you love—or even once loved—your partner, this is a heartrending choice. If you are married and/or have children with your partner, you are well aware of all the emotional and financial implications this decision will have on all the elements of your life. Even if you are single and you and your partner have been together only a short time, you may still worry about how much pain you might experience as you begin to extricate yourself from this emotional involvement.

Here are some suggestions on how to arrive at and best handle this decision for yourself.

STAY GROUNDED IN REALITY

As you make decisions about yourself and your relationship, it's essential that you keep your feet firmly planted on Mother

Earth. Relationships with narcissists are inevitably fraught with fantasy, illusion, and delusion. Remember little Orphan Annie singing about "Tomorrow," as the day on which dreams would come true. Narcissistic relationships always seem to hold out the promise of better and more idyllic tomorrows. These relationships are always filled with unrealized and unfulfilled potential. It's all about tomorrow.

We've spoken to more than a few people who said that they were afraid of leaving a narcissistic relationship because they feared that "tomorrow" would be when all the promise and promises—spoken and unspoken—of the relationship would materialize, and they would miss their chance.

We typically fall in love with narcissists because we are swept up in the web of illusion they weave, and we stay with narcissists because we continue to hope against hope that our dreams will eventually be fulfilled. Sometimes our dreams are so modest that we don't immediately identify them as dreams. For example, all Becky wants is for her husband to stop getting angry at her; all Austin wants is for his wife to spend time with him and the kids. If you are thinking about walking away from a narcissist, one of the first things you have to evaluate is whether your dreams, no matter how modest, have a chance of being fulfilled.

Narcissists fill us up and wipe us out with their fantasies and their promises and their idealization. You need to be able to take a long, hard look at your situation. Stay in the here and now and take a look at the history of your relationship and what has transpired. Take a look at the present, and make a realistic decision about what you think the future will be. Just remember: reality is your friend. One of the things you need to do is evaluate your own emotional history and vulnerability. We think it's pretty safe to say that nobody with a rock-solid sense of self and a good support system gets enmeshed with a toxic narcissist. Having a relationship with a narcissist always means leaving at least a little bit of yourself behind.

When you love a narcissist, you know the kind of perilous ride he/she can take you on: One minute the person you love can make you feel wonderful; the next he/she can make you feel like you have no value and don't exist. Everything gets askew and you begin to feel as though only this person has the power to make you feel whole, and nothing else gives you any sustenance whatsoever. It's as though you have been caught up in a web from which you can't entangle yourself. Reality is the way you get free of these feelings. Trust us, once you are able to move back and take a realistic look at your situation, you will see that the web you are enmeshed in is illusory. When you get free of it, you will feel as though you are coming out of a dream.

Try to find activities that put some psychological space between you and the narcissist you love. Take a course or an adult-ed class. Pursue some self-improvement activity such as a workout program. Is there a political group you would like to join or a cause you would like to help? Getting involved with activities that take your mind away from your narcissist and his/her problems can help you stay grounded and realistic. This can also help you gain some perspective.

Find a way to create a support system of friends and family to help you stay grounded in the here and now. Ask them to help you develop some reality checks. Don't allow your relationship or your partner to make you feel divorced from the real world. Look at your partner with open eyes and see the reality, as opposed to the promise or the potential. Don't be afraid to see the truth.

RECOGNIZE THE DIFFERENCE BETWEEN NARCISSISTIC ISSUES AND TOXIC NARCISSISM

Here's something you have to realistically decide for yourself: does your partner have *some* narcissistic issues, or is your partner a destructive, full-blown narcissist?

It's obvious that the answer to that question can make a big difference in how you should be thinking about your relationship. Two large mistakes that people often make about their relationships have to do with going to extremes and incorrectly evaluating the degree to which their partners are narcissistic.

- **Mistake Number One: Viewing an average, 21st century, spoiled person as being totally narcissistic.**

Jennie, for example, thinks her live-in boyfriend, Patrick, is totally narcissistic because he takes up more closet space than she does, refuses to help her do the dishes or empty the kitty litter, and can't stop talking about his new job. Jennie has visited a few Web sites about narcissism, has read portions of two books about the disorder, and is prepared to make a personal diagnosis. Jennie may be right in thinking that Patrick is a little selfish and a little self-involved. However, Jennie is failing to take into consideration all the ways in which Patrick is well-intentioned and sympathetic to her needs. Jennie is confusing narcissism with laziness. What Jennie is complaining about is that Patrick isn't perfect. Indeed, none of us are.

We think it's important that none of us get hung up on the label *narcissistic* and attach it to every person and every situation that doesn't go along with what we want. In fact, when we do that, we may well be more deserving of the label than the person we are pointing at.

- **Mistake Number Two: Going into denial about how destructive and how narcissistic a partner really is.**

On the other extreme are the many, many men and women who seem unable to appropriately label a partner's brutally narcissistic behavior. Remember that narcissists tend to present two separate and distinct sides to their personalities. One minute they can appear deflated and extremely sensitive and vulnerable; the next, they are inflated and seem incapable of noticing anyone except themselves.

When you love a narcissist, it's easy to put more emphasis on the insecure aspects of their personality. We feel most connected to them when they show us their vulnerability. Because this side of their personality resonates loudest with us, we make excuses for them to ourselves and to others. We think things like, "I know Charlie is unfaithful/dishonest/spending all our money/ abusive/angry all the time, and doesn't seem to want to do anything to please me, but last week when he poured his heart out to me, and told me he was sorry, there were tears in his eyes. I know he loves me and doesn't want to lose me." We say things like, "Don't pay any attention to Natalie. I know she was rude and mean to you and your family, and I know she can't stop talking about herself, but she's really not like that. If you knew her like I do, you'd know that there are two sides to her personality."

You are never going to be able to be realistic about your situation if you keep making excuses and denying your partner's hurtful behavior. There are certain hallmarks of narcissistic behavior. One of the most glaring is the difficulty narcissists have in feeling empathy for anyone but themselves. Ask yourself:

• Is my partner able to understand how much he/she is hurting others, including me?
• Is my partner able to care about how much he/she is hurting others, including me?

If you have a partner who consistently puts you down or is being emotionally abusive, physically abusive, unfaithful, or chronically dishonest, you are probably in love with a narcissist. If you have a partner whose need for attention is so great that it controls your life, then you are probably in love with a narcissist. If that same partner refuses to discuss or modify his/her behavior, you are almost definitely in love with a narcissist. We know that nothing we can tell you will make you stop loving this person. We do think, however, that if you are able to at least recognize and understand the nature of your partner's problem, it will help you become more realistic about what you can and cannot do to make life better for yourself.

RECOGNIZE THAT IT TAKES TWO PEOPLE TO MAKE A RELATIONSHIP WORK

You can only make a relationship work if your partner is willing to do some work with you. Yes, there is a lot that you can do to make yourself more comfortable within your relationship, but there are certain situations that are almost impossible to handle. For example, there is no effective way to deal with a partner who is physically abusive. You have to remove yourself from the situation and protect yourself accordingly. Other behavior that is intolerable includes chronic infidelity, abusive anger, deceit, sadism, manipulation, and a complete lack of cooperation. Obviously it goes without saying that if your narcissistic partner is emotionally or physically abusive of your children, you must protect them; your children are your priority.

Sometimes men and women make decisions about their relationships that go something like this: "I'm going to go home and tell Jane/Jim that I truly love her/him. Then I'm going to stop nagging, demanding, whining, complaining, or crying about anything that happens. I've decided that I'm going to make my relationship work—no matter what." These same men and women then go home and do their darndest. The only problem is that Jane or Jim are not on the same page. Neither Jane nor Jim change in the slightest, no matter what their partners may do or not do. Oh sure, they might be happy that they are not being nagged. They appreciate the calm; they appreciate the absence of strife, but it doesn't alter their behavior. That's because Jane and Jim are narcissists. This means that they are behaving the way they do because of the way they are. It has nothing to do with what you are doing or not doing.

GET HELP AND GET SUPPORT!

This is probably the most important piece of advice we can give you. If you are in love with a narcissist, speaking to a mental heath professional is frequently a necessary step that has to be taken. You need support to help you sort things out. Somebody with professional experience can often help you evaluate what's going on in your relationship. Books like this one can't substitute for help that is both personal and professional. If you are experiencing the symptoms of anxiety or depression, it's absolutely essential that you consult an accredited professional—the sooner the better.

Some of you have may have turned to the Internet to learn more about what to do about your narcissistic partners. Within the last year, the amount of information on the Internet about narcissism appears to have tripled. There is some good and even great information. There is also a ton of stuff that can be described as extreme at best, and we don't think the Internet is always a realistic and viable substitute for professional help, either.

Some of you may not be in a financial position to start spending money on therapy or counseling. We've been there, and we understand. Nonetheless, before you decide that you can't afford it, you might want to check out the possibility of short-term therapy. Unlike traditional therapy, short-term therapy is limited in terms of time. It can be directed at a specific goal, as in helping someone reach a decision. Some therapists are willing to see clients for crisis intervention or short-term therapy, lasting anywhere from a few sessions to several months. There are a wide variety of short-term therapy techniques available. You might want to check it out on the Internet to see if any of them appeal to you.

Another possible way of getting support as well as insight into your relationship is to become involved with a support group such as Co-Dependents Anonymous, or CoDA as it is known. CoDA is sometimes thought of as a support group for partners of people with alcohol or substance abuse issues. However, over the years it has grown to include people with other kinds of relationship problems. This is a Twelve Step program, and if CoDA's message resonates with you, at the very least it will help you think more about the relationships in your life. We know many people who credit CoDA with giving them enormous support as well as great insight and strength into how to develop more fulfilling relationships. Again, look this up online, and you will be able to get the address of meetings near you. If your partner does have substance abuse issues, don't forget AlAnon. When you become a member of many of these groups, you can find immediate support and understanding; often you will be assigned a sponsor to help you through the rocky times.

Many communities have other types of support and counseling available that are either free or have a minimal cost. Look for organizations designed to help survivors of physical, mental, or emotional abuse.

There are other support groups, which you might find information about online. If you belong to a religious organization, your spiritual leader may have some advice about how and where to find inexpensive counseling options or groups that you can join. This is a time when you should do whatever possible to stay calm and centered. Don't discount practices such as yoga and/or meditation as ways of healing. All of these may help you gain perspective and clarity. Many YMCA/YWCA organizations and community centers offer meditation and yoga programs.

No one thing may provide you with an ideal amount of resolve, inner strength, and clarity right now, but don't be afraid to try several complimentary practices simultaneously. There is nothing that says you can't take advantage of yoga classes, meditation workshops, and therapy at the same time. Do everything you can to get calm, strong, and centered. Whatever decision you make about your relationship, don't become discouraged if there is some backsliding. Just pick yourself up and continue back in the direction you want to go.